ᐊᔥ | Views from the Intersection

                    to apprehend
The point of intersection of the timeless
With time, is an occupation for the saint—
No occupation either, but something given
And taken, in a lifetime's death in love,
Ardour and selflessness and self-surrender.

                    —*T.S. Eliot*
                    "The Dry Salvages"

Views from the Intersection

Poems by
Catherine Barry

Meditations by
Virginia Ramey Mollenkott

CROSSROAD ۽ NEW YORK

For our mothers:
Gertrude Rose Barry
and
May Lotz Ramey

1984
The Crossroad Publishing Company
370 Lexington Avenue, New York, N.Y. 10017

Printed in the United States of America

Library of Congress Cataloging in Publication Data

Mollenkott, Virginia.
  Views from the intersection.
  1. Meditations.   I. Barry, Catherine.   II. Title.
BV4832.2.M555   1984   242   83-23150
ISBN 0-8245-0634-0 (pbk.)

The epigraph is taken from "The Dry Salvages"
in *Four Quartets*, copyright 1943 by T.S. Eliot;
renewed 1971 by Esme Valerie Eliot. Reprinted
by permission of Harcourt Brace Jovanovich, Inc.

⤶ | Contents

⟆ | What Views? What Intersection? And Why?

When I am interacting with audiences, people frequently ask me about my inner experience. What does prayer feel like to me? How do I envision God? And I understand that their curiosity is more than idle. It is important to one's own growth to learn how others are handling their inner process, the life of the spirit. Indeed, breaking out of isolation and into community is one way of defining the religious impulse.

We who love literature love it partly for that very reason: reading enables us to look at life through the eyes of someone else, to feel life's vicissitudes on the pulse of another person, and thus to sense our connectedness and even our mortal inter-indebtedness.

When I was young, I had such a difficult time separating (even briefly) from those I loved that I anxiously watched movies and read books about parting. I consciously trained myself with whatever insights I could glean about how other people handled the moments of "goodbye" and the days that followed. And it worked; my anxiety lessened. I've been using literature as a soul-gymnasium ever since. Although, of course, training in how to cope is only one dimension of experiencing literature, it is an important dimension.

Views from the Intersection is intended to carry its readers into the consciousness of two contemporary Christian feminists (that is, believers in human equality), the poet a Roman Catholic, the essayist a Protestant of fundamentalist background. I first met Catherine Barry when she was chairing the Foreign Language Department at William Paterson College and I was chairing the English Department. Our jobs required our presence on the dean's Humanities Division Council, where the work could hardly have been more mundane and less inspiring. I liked Catherine's wit from the start; but liking deepened into friendship when we discovered each other's feminism and theocentric world view.

When Catherine showed me her poems, I was drawn to the way they provided new figures of speech for me, fresh ways of imaging God, people, animals, plants, books, and various other aspects of being alive. I soon realized that Catherine was depicting mystical experience, and doing so in the only way a contemporary feminist can possibly do it: by saluting the holiness of ordinary, concrete, everyday experience. Annie Dillard entitled one of her books *Holy the Firm*—and indeed, if that which is firm (what we call matter) is not holy, then how can we humanly embodied people hope to connect with the divine without devaluing embodiment? To paraphrase St. John, if we say we love God's essence which we have not seen, yet cannot love God as manifested in ourselves and other creatures we have seen, we are liars and the truth is not in us.

Yet when the chips are really down, it is difficult to believe in the validity of one's own spiritual experience! I can instantly recognize tremendous torment and agony in someone else's life as quite possibly the dark night of the soul. But when such torments visit me, I dare not hope for so profound a significance. Looking at someone else, I can see without the distraction of myriads of mundane irritations and complex interrelationships within my consciousness. Yet unless I learn to recognize the holy within the experience I call my own, with all its possibly skewed perceptions, where within the human condition will I ever be able to meet and relate to God? Here or nowhere. Now or never. Now, here, and in no other place or time.

In her book *Women's Reality*, psychotherapist Anne Wilson Schaef describes the difference between the way women think (the Female System) and the White Male System that predominates in our culture. In the White Male System, she explains, "living in tune with God means getting in tune with something outside of the self.... In order to be attuned to God, one must learn to deny or transcend the self ... strive to be what one is not." But in the Female System, "living in tune with [G]od means being in tune with what one already is.... One must only stay in tune with one's process to remain attuned to [G]od. Our true selves are never in conflict with [G]od. And [G]od is not *just* our process and [G]od *is* our process."

Clearly, by Schaef's definition, Catherine Barry's poetry is Female-System poetry. Like Catherine, however, I would not draw the line between male and female thought-systems so much as between the patriarchal and feminist consciousness. I have met women who have bought completely into the White Male System, and I have met men who have opted out of it and into a Liberation Perspective that is an amalgam of the Female and Third World Systems. So I think that Catherine's mystical poems, and the meditations inspired by them, will appeal to men in the process of liberating themselves as well as to women involved in their own internal process.

Mystical poetry is inevitably difficult poetry. Poetry itself, and especially modern poetry, tends to be difficult for many people. Add to that the intensely individualistic nature of the mystical experience—it is simultaneously the most universal and most individualistic of experiences—and the problem is compounded. Just as each person looks different physically, each of us interacts somewhat differently with the Divine Spirit that is the basis of our own being and every being. And each of us draws on our own intellectual and imaginative history as we try to put into words what has happened to us. For that reason I have explained Catherine's frame of reference for each poem—who Robbe Grillet is, for instance, and what his work means to Catherine (in "Bourbon and Words"). Without that information, some of her puns and internal strategies for coping with an academic bore would be lost to us. And without sharing these specifics of Catherine's world (her relevant history) we cannot enter into the timeless and universal aspects of her experience. Time does indeed intersect with eternity. But to attempt to enter directly and exclusively into eternity is to reject the human condition. It is to abandon responsibility for the world we live in. It is to be drugged by the dehumanized and dehumanizing abstractions of White Male System theology.

To illustrate: Catherine Barry is not content to generalize about Platonic Ideas and resurrection bodies. She describes an ordinary flesh-blood-and-fur calico cat prowling a hill behind her home, wrestles with the embodiment of Platonic theories in that very cat, and comes up with some very alive, "very surprising fur" ("In the Forests of the Night"). Responding to her poem, my mind flashes through William Blake and Sir Thomas Browne and Henry David Thoreau, all of them white males, none of them trapped in the White Male System. They in turn stimulate my own imaginings. As Robert Browning said concerning artistic embodiments, "God uses us to help each other so/ Lending our minds out."

In short, *Views from the Intersection* encapsulates moments when for Catherine Barry, time has intersected eternity. It also encapsulates moments when Catherine Barry's tough, unsentimental vision has inspired my spirit to its own experiences at the intersection. It is our hope that reading *Views* will do more than provide insights about Christian feminist spirituality and twentieth-century mysticism, though it should certainly do both. We hope that our readers will be stimulated again and again to open themselves to their personal birthright: direct experience of God at the intersection of the timeless with time.

—Virginia Ramey Mollenkott

◦§ | The Space

The space to be for now
Is not here, nor there,
But between the shape of the world
And the soul spark.
Here means the edges of sharp, spare,
Full and narrow
Like notebooks, jots, columns, tittles,
And the sky between high rises.
There means at the edge of light.
Nail your tongue and feet and fingers
Firm in the space
Not here, not there
Which is the same as saying
In neither and both at this one time.

MEDITATION

T. S. Eliot wrote that living at "the intersection of the timeless with time" is the occupation of a saint. I'd like to be a saint, wouldn't you? Not so much in the technical sense of being canonized by church authorities, but rather in Eliot's sense of being constantly in touch with eternal values (the timeless) even while going about the often routine and sometimes painful tasks of the here and now —tasks like combating the unjust systems that oppress God's children. To work for world peace and justice without slipping away from serene rest at the center of ourselves: that, indeed, is the occupation of a saint.

I believe that every Christian is eligible for that kind of saint-hood, for several reasons. First, because St. Paul so frequently addressed his epistles to all the saints in Rome, Corinth, Ephesus, Philippi, or wherever, implying that all the members of each congregation were "called to be saints." And secondly, because St. John wrote in no uncertain terms (1 John 3:2; 4:16) that our membership in God's family is *now*, and therefore that the nature of God (which is Love) is intended to be our vital experience during this life on earth. Not just in the sweet bye and bye, but right here and right now!

What Catherine does in "The Space" is try to define the precise location of "the intersection of the timeless with time." Where does eternity touch down into time? How does our ordinary time-bound consciousness take on the eternal dimension? The space in which this must occur is "not here, nor there"—that is, it is neither wholly material (like notebook entries or the constraint of high-rise apartment buildings) nor wholly spiritual and ethereal (like the "soul spark" and "the edge of light").

Why does Catherine's heart tell her (and us) to "Nail your tongue and feet and fingers/ Firm in the space/ Not here, not there"? Because speaking, moving, and touching with a constant awareness of eternity in our words, actions, and relationships requires a firm and constantly renewed act of the will. It requires no less than a *nailing*, a determined refusal to be drawn either into total immersion in this-worldliness or into complacently pietistic other-worldliness. "Not here, not there."

To fulfill our calling as saints here in the twentieth century, we must learn to be oriented neither toward the earth nor toward eternity, and yet at the same time to be oriented both toward the earth and toward eternity: "neither and both at this one time." That is the space into which we must nail ourselves.

Any similarity to a cross lifted up between heaven and earth is purely intentional.

ᜪ | Bourbon and Words

(at an old-fashioned cocktail party)

If the mouth keeps on shooting book bullets
At the bars of your little prison
Inside the professor's living room,
Robbe-Grillet it:
Freeze the cube and circle letters
On your rectangle teeth.
Better still: run fast into your brain
And fast rewind.
Turn the amber glass in Words' waving hand
Into a madeleine.
Ride rocking in a madeleine boat
With Rousseau off Ile-St.-Pierre.
Now try fast forward
To the black hole whimpering out—
Words and his book will end.
Or get it on hold
At Eckhart and the gentle Orient—
Words and the world are nothing,
Words, the beloved
In the Beloved's cosmic smile.
But be prepared:
Great purring jailer is coming
With more amber liquid
And a lot more shot.

MEDITATION

Every occupation has its boring stretches. One of the hazards of being a college professor is having to endure academic cocktail parties at which pedantic colleagues seize the opportunity to impress you with their brilliance. The question in "Bourbon and Words" is how to live through such a monologue without losing all patience and acting downright rude.

Six possibilities emerge during the course of the poem. The first is to imagine the whole scene—yourself, the room you're standing in on the second floor of some professor's house, the other people, and "Words" (the person who is peppering you with pedantic "book bullets")—to imagine all of this as part of a huge geometric design, all cubes, circles, and rectangles. Robbe-Grillet was a leader in the late-1950's French literary movement called the New Novel, which emphasized paring down reality to its essential "thingness," its material and geometrical skeleton, minus metaphor and minus metaphysics. So one way to keep from exploding at the professional bore is simply to "Robbe-Grillet" the whole incident: to distance yourself by imagining yourself part of a geometrical arrangement.

A second, bettter possibility springs from the first. You can treat your brain like a tape recorder, setting it for fast forward and then fast rewind, escaping the stifling moment by transcending the trap of chronology. To help yourself accomplish this feat, you can focus on the cocktail in the hand of "Words" (the bore), imagining that the drink has turned into a "madeleine," a seashell-shaped French pastry made famous in Proust's *Remembrance of Things Past*. On one occasion, dipping his pastry into some tea had triggered remembrance of his own past; therefore Proust made the madeleine into a symbol of such retrieval of both our conscious and unconscious memories. So in an impossibly boring situation you can always escape by imaginatively resurrecting the past within yourself.

Which leads to a third possibility: you can also "Ride rocking in a madeleine [shell-shaped] boat / With Rousseau off Ile-St.-Pierre." In his latter years Jean Jacques Rousseau became paranoid and spent a lot of time in withdrawn solitude, boating just off the coast of the French Island of St. Peter. Remembering him suggests that mindless withdrawal is another way to cope.

When that wears down, you can push the fast-forward button again, projecting yourself all the way into the future when, according to modern astronomical theory, our solar system will be sucked into a black hole. This scenario provides the distinct comfort of remembering that the person and all the words that are boring you will certainly be brought to a conclusion sooner or later. And as T. S. Eliot put it, the end will come "not with a bang, but a whimper."

A fifth possibility arises out of the black hole theory with its inevitable speculations about what might await us "out there" beyond space as we know it. You can switch your mind onto "hold"; that is, you can get it into a sense of "no-time" or eternity, by contemplating the insights of the mystical tradition, both Eastern ("the gentle Orient") and Western (represented by the medieval German mystic Meister Eckhart). Through remembrance that the things which are not seen are eternal, you can reach the liberation of knowing that what you perceive with your physical eyes is only temporal. Therefore, "Words and the world are nothing." And you realize that in the real world of the unseen and eternal, even your wretched pedant is a member of the mystical Body of Christ: "Words [is] the beloved/ In the Beloved's [Christ's] cosmic smile." Or in Oriental terms, you realize that even "Words" is part of the Buddha nature, or the Tao, or the One.

No sooner have you arrived at this inspiring insight, however, than you see your host, the "Great purring jailer," arriving with "a lot more shot" of bourbon. Fuel, alas, for yet another hour of tedium! The final word, "shot," is of course a pun to remind us of the "book bullets" we have been coping with throughout. Other puns include the name Robbe-Grillet (grill it) and the "cube" which is both a geometric form and an ice cube to play with in your mouth as further distraction from the anguish of boredom. These puns point up a sixth and final coping mechanism that has been implied by the format of the whole poem: you can always provide your own internal entertainment by toying with language and ideas while apparently being absorbed in dull academic monologues.

Working out our salvation almost always takes place under less-than-perfect circumstances, and all of us could probably name our own equivalent of the academic cocktail party. Our solutions are frequently less than perfect, too. Honest confrontation with our own humanity, as in "Bourbon and Words," may ultimately be the most spiritual course of action.

✒ | For Joan Her First Time

To have a child is at last
To chart with certainty
The tracking of plush monsters
In the kitchen.
To take responsibility
For the secret life of poodles.
This time round to hear
Why things squeak in the night,
To smell why birds fly,
And see why wet is not dry.
Lovely to know for sure at last.
Only one small catch:
Children tell and cannot know;
Their mothers know and cannot tell.

MEDITATION

The limitations of the human condition—how we would like to rise
above them, and yet we cannot! As someone remarked concerning
mystical experience, "Those who tell do not know; those who know
cannot tell." The mother in her first experience of motherhood at
last intuits the essential nature of things she only chattered about
when she was a child. Watching her baby's experience and remembering her own, she understands her child's acts of imagination. For the child, and for a mother peering through her child's

eyes, "plush monsters" roam around the kitchen. As mother, a woman achieves a wholistic understanding of her own act of imagination as she interprets for her child the subjective emotions of the family's pet poodle ("See his sad face? He doesn't *like* it if you pull his tail!").

This time around, the mother thinks she knows "with certainty" the underlying rationale for things that were only face-value facts in her childhood: sounds in the night, birds flying, wetness as opposed to dryness. But human limitation reasserts itself, for when the mother actually tries to explain the things she is so sure she understands, she cannot do so.

For all that we adults think we know, there remains an ineluctable mystery behind even the most commonplace realities. We can let ourselves be frustrated by this mystery, or we can rejoice in it. But one thing is certain: we must live with it.

ᵛᵍ | About to Shake Hands

The first man's hand I saw
Was red rock,
Hard wrinkles pressed up
From the vein juices,
Such meeting that
Of Poem and Mind,
My father's hand.
Yours with long fingers
Projected along the wall of light
Between us, more like
A hard boned starfish
Than a rock—
Yours touches his and his yours,
Where rock and starfish greet,
Strange Gemini, in the sky
Of before and after in this tiny now.

MEDITATION

Great is the power of the human mind. In it the memories of a long-dead father can mingle and merge and even form new relationships with thoughts of a living friend. The father's hand, although a rock, is able to float in this special sea—literally impossible, of course, but possible because of the transformations mind can achieve. The father's hand is both red and gray, with the peasant's rock-hardness of surface. And the surface is wrinkled by the efforts and energies spawned by the blood. In itself the hand forms a marriage between concept and embodiment. By contrast, the friend's more delicate hand is not like a rock but like a wild starfish. And even though the friend is not dead but alive, still it is between him and herself that Catherine senses a "wall of light." What wall? For those with eyes to see it, between even contemporaries and friends stands a barrier of mystery, a separation to be penetrated only by communion and understanding.

Amazingly enough, both friend and father can float together like the twins of the zodiac, the Gemini, in a mental sea that is also a sky—and a poem. Father long dead and living friend reach toward each other, about to shake hands in the sea/sky poem/mind of their daughter/friend. Fearfully and wonderfully made, the human mind melds past and present, image and poem, there and here, dead and living, time and eternity.

✒ | In the Forests of the Night

Is there a true you-cat?
I don't mean is there catness.
I mean is there a calico dainty rage
Realer than you who play dark Africa here
On my tiny hill till the dark
Calls you back to dark me inside.

Small tiger burning bright,
I know who made thee,
Or at least I see you made.
I am asking, is there truer you?

If my fingers will not die,
But feel forever their true fingering,
I will never stroke a catness,
But, I do expect,
Some very surprising fur
You'll be that's you.

MEDITATION

We are buried a natural body, we are raised a spiritual body. So
says 1 Corinthians 15:44. But what is the very essence of any being?
What will the resurrection body be like? What will eternal and
essential embodiment look like? What will it feel like?

Imagining a tiger burning bright in the forests of the night, William Blake asked a cosmic question. Did the same Creator who made the tender lamb also produce the untamed, beautiful, and terrifying tumults of the tiger? Catherine, watching an ordinary cat prowling the little hill behind her home, also ponders a cosmic question, but a much different one. What sort of ultimate self may lie behind the cat's playful and alert fur?

She flatly rejects the easy answers of Platonism. It is not the Idea of "catness," not a philosophical abstraction, that interests her. For after all, real fingers cannot stroke a "catness." Will human fingers remain true fingers after death and resurrection? Will they remember their ability to feel? If so, then that cat out there on the hillside is still going to feel like something furry to them. But what *kind* of furry? Clearly, a surprise must be in store for us all.

When evening deepens, Catherine can no longer see her miniature tiger playing dark Africa on the hillside. But because she can remember what she has seen and wondered, the cat moves inward, into the mysterious darkness of her own inner being. "We carry all Africa and her prodigies within us," exclaimed Sir Thomas Browne. And Henry David Thoreau wondered why so many people were clamoring to explore the still uncharted areas on the world map, when so many dark continents remained unexplored within the individual soul. But what, exactly, *is* that human soul? What *is* that spiritual body?

The questions that tantalize our humanity will never be answered until we can feel with our eternal fingertips a tiny tiger's very surprising fur.

✍ | Mid-Winter

Here, there are no birds to speak of—
No three-pronged remembrance
Of a friend's search
For survival after flight.
Here, there's not one tree.
I might be a puzzled sparrow
Torn between white sky and ground.

MEDITATION

Andrew Marvell wrote about feeling claustrophobic pressure as time's winged chariot pushes him toward the terrifyingly empty desert of vast eternity. That's one of the moods experienced by people who fear death and are magnetized by their own eagerness for human experience. Catherine writes of a much more passive mood: a sense of being nowhere, being lost and empty, being suspended in a blank-white landscape, neither fully engaged by time nor fully immersed in eternity.

A sterile snow burdens all the trees. No birds are searching the frigid ground for the food that would spell their survival; not even any bird tracks leave their mark upon the snow. Only the speaker and the empathetic reader are there, like sparrows somehow left behind for the winter, alone in a frozen landscape. In such a mood we feel torn, because on the one hand we are attached to the endings that are always part of time's process. And on the other hand we are attracted by the different, never-ending continuum of the eternal. From this perspective, time and eternity, spirit and body, life and death seem to be opposites, poles apart, and we find ourselves neither there nor here and thoroughly uncomfortable with that fact. We are "torn between white sky and ground." We feel bleak. We feel mid-winter. But if we are wise, we do not deny our feelings. We simply feel them. And we endure.

An Evergreen Shrub Sold to Me at "Arcadian Gardens," Wayne, New Jersey

"To my outer man, creatures taste like creatures . . .
to my inner man, they taste like gifts of God. . . .
and to my innermost being, they are not like gifts
of God, but like forever and evermore."
—*Meister Eckhart*

Through my glasses and my window
This shrub tastes like itself:
Late afternoon leaves of summer,
Impatient fingers upsetting clipped fist order—
Green mouths crying
More food, more drink, please,
Before the sun shuts down.

But to my heart's retina
The shrub is already
Wrapped green-ribboned heart
Catching me home this afternoon
For surprise birthday partying.

Still I am at inmost
The inmost shrub and it is I:
Unending oval past and future green,
Veined shooting life
Burst through time's hole,
Being a green eye always
And becoming always leaf.

MEDITATION

Meister Eckhart identifies three levels of relating to even the most mundane objects. The first is the external, objective level at which each thing is to be respected for its otherness, its own special flavor, its uniqueness. The second is the subjective level, at which things are perceived according to their meaning to the perceiver. In the God-centered mind, things are valued at this level as the gifts of the Creator.

Thus far Eckhart has described human levels of perception that are fairly universal, though of course keenness of appreciation varies greatly between one individual and another. The third level Eckhart mentions, however, is a type of awareness known only to religious or natural mystics: the level at which subject-object differentiation breaks down and the perceiver feels his or her oneness with that which is perceived. As a Christian mystic who knows that his innermost being is hidden in God through Christ, Eckhart names this innermost identification "forever and evermore."

Poet Marianne Moore said that the task of the poet is above all to be concrete: to build "imaginary gardens with real toads in them." Consequently, Catherine embodies Eckhart's insight by choosing just one "creature," a shrub she purchased at a garden store in Wayne, New Jersey. The name of the nursery, Arcadian Gardens, is an exotic one, since Greek Arcadia is a symbol famous in poetry for all that is rustic, pastoral, peaceful, simple, and the like.

Looking out the window at the now-planted shrub—with both

her eyeglasses and the window pane reminding us that human perception is always "through a glass darkly"—Catherine first experiences the shrub as uniquely and concretely other from herself. Although when first purchased the shrub was a perfectly trimmed fist-shaped oval, now some of the newest shoots have disturbed the symmetry by their eager growth and reaching toward the sun.

On another level, to the eye of the heart, the shrub is not simply a shrub, but a surprise birthday gift tied with green ribbon. In Christian art, green represents hope, fertility, regeneration, victory, and triumph over death. But how can a shrub one has purchased and planted become a gift and a surprise? Easily: the surprise gift lies in the sudden cleansing of perception, whereby what was only a shrub transforms into a bush burning with the presence of its Creator. An ordinary summer afternoon leaps into a divine visitation.

But there is more. Her attention focused on the shrub, Catherine loses her awareness of separate identity to become united with the shrub's essential being. (By Christ all things consist, according to Colossians 1:17). Poet and shrub unite in an unending oval, not only coming from Life but also moving toward Life. (The oval halo, or mandorla, a womb-like symbol of eternal perfection, is often used in Christian paintings to enclose an important holy figure).

Together forming a single green mandorla, poet and shrub burst for one surprising second through time's hole, the entrance into eternity. On that level they are simultaneously always being and always becoming, always the contemplative eye that triumphs over time's vicissitudes, yet always the leaf that grows and dissolves and changes in unending process. In that astonishing instant the ordinary shrub is not only itself, not only a gift of God, but also forever and evermore.

৺ | Same Game New

I thought to go back to "Go"
To see the gate again.
My point was to nail my sight
To one fine screw on the strait hinge
Hanging on time before and after.
But instead I became myself the gate
Swinging between the forgotten
And the fading.

MEDITATION

What is the nature of my own consciousness? Might I be able to
grasp it by returning to my birth-moment, my own beginning as
the consciousness I call myself? Curious, the speaker attempts to
roll her own consciousness back to "Go," to the primal, to the genesis of awareness. She hopes to apprehend her own consciousness
by sheer intensity of focus, nailing her sight to any single aspect of
that gate which forms the hinge between the unfamiliar time before birth (the forgotten) and the more familiar but always fading
moments afterwards.

Her attempt is frustrated, however, by the discovery that she
herself is the gate, the subject of her own consciousness, the game
that is being played. She herself is the gate impaled between time
and eternity. She herself is the swinging hinge, the strait, the narrow place between the time before birth and after death. There is
no "fine screw" to hold onto, no experience that will stand still
long enough to focus awareness upon.

Even when paying the most careful conscious attention, we are still split off from the unconscious level that makes up so much of our human reality. It is only in the moment that we cease to worry about heightened consciousness that we are home-free, united to our own genesis, having become ourselves the gate. But we remain frustrated in the attempt to *see* the gate. We cannot see the gate for the simple reason that we are the gate. We are therefore the game that is simultaneously always the same and always new.

So at the deepest level we are always a mystery to ourselves, as others are a mystery to us and we to them. In acceptance of this mystery lies sanity, realism, humility, and peace.

✒ | Hope Is the Smell of God

The nose is the nosiest.

Even when chairs and tables
Have come to dust with the dust
That lies on them,
The smell of lost century rooms
Still won't go.

Smell runs ahead, too, for our other parts.
Old dog sniffer gets friend or foe
First and right in the wind or lees.

Only my nose makes it through the wall
Between myself and me
And comes back with the smell of God
Into today's half light.

MEDITATION

What are the internal counterparts of the five senses? Tradition-
ally, faith is the counterpart of seeing and hearing ("Faith comes
by hearing"; "Look unto me and be ye saved"). Love is the counterpart of taste and touch ("O taste and see that the Lord is good,"
"that which our hands have handled of the word of God"). But the
internal counterpart of hope is the sense of smell, that sense which
according to novelist Marcel Proust is the most lasting of all the
senses and therefore best facilitates the recall of memories.

The nose, Catherine suggests, is the most probing and curious of human sensors. Turning backward, the nose can sense the mustiness of an old room long after all its furniture has moldered away. Looking forward, whether approached from the windy or quiet side, the nose accurately alerts us to the presence of our friend or foe. Looking inward, only the internal counterpart of the sense of smell—only hope—is able to penetrate the mysterious wall between our everyday consciousness and the deepest, truest Self where God dwells. And therefore only hope can come back to the ordinary world bearing with it the smell of God. It is that whiff of God's presence that introduces hope even into the half-light of ordinary everyday awareness.

ᵅᔥ | Christmas Morning (to My Self)

"Mine are the heavens and mine is the earth."
—*John of the Cross*

I saw you come down
Darkening the stair,
Moving velvet in the light,
Done with sleep and descending to the dream,
Straight to the double open doors
And on to the Christmas tree.
It will be all there as you had been wished—
All is yours: Easter Island,
The islands, easters, and the Easter.

MEDITATION

Like many other mystics, St. John of the Cross experienced an expansive sense of well-being as the Beloved of God—a sense that because he was united to the divine nature, the heavens and earth and all the universe belonged to him. Although at first this attitude can look like the height of egotism, it is actually the opposite of egotism, since true mystics rejoice that what is true for them is true also for anyone anywhere who is willing to undergo a change of perception, a dying-into-life.

In this poem Catherine envisions her deep Self, her authentic being which is grounded in God's Being, descending the stairs like a beautiful woman dressed in velvet. (Yet of course the inner being is also always a child. Remember the childhood thrill of racing down the stairs on Christmas morning to catch a glimpse of the gifts waiting underneath the Christmas tree?) In this case, a truly stupendous gift awaits the alerted Self: Easter. What a celebration of birth! Resurrection Life!

Catherine uses "sleep" and "dream" in the same sense as St. John of the Cross. To be asleep is to be wholly invested in mundane affairs. To descend to the dream is to go deeper into Reality, to begin to come alive spiritually. (At best, we see through a glass darkly; at best, we dream. Our visions of the ultimate, as Shakespeare wrote, are inevitably "such stuff/ As dreams are made on, and our little life/ Is rounded with a sleep.")

Once we begin to come alive to the depths of Reality, like contented children we will find the fulfilment of all our wishes under the Christmas tree. (When I say to God, "Be it unto me according to Thy will," and thus fuse my will to God's will, there is no way that that will can be thwarted. The universe will certainly *selve itself*, I can be sure of that!) Here is the reason Catherine uses the passive voice when she says "It will be all there as you *had been* wished," rather than saying "as you had wished." In eternity, and in the Eternal Now, we know as we have been known. We wish and will as we have been wished and willed. One of the implications of the passive usage is that the distinction between the divine will and human will has been transcended. Another is that our own Self is one of the gifts that is prepared for us under the Christmas tree of God's grace. We must accept our Selves along with all the other gifts. Helping people achieve the divine gift— notice the paradox—of Self-acceptance is one of the most important things we can be about.

And the gifts of grace include everything! Easter Island evokes the mystery that surrounds the fabulous statues on the Polynesian island, and thus represents all the mysteries surrounding the past, both my own and that of the human race. In union with God, all these mysteries are mine. So are "the islands"—both everyday experiences and the sense of God's presence that may flash out of them. (St. John of the Cross wrote, "My beloved [Christ] is the

Islands.") The "easters" are the small resurrections of everyday life, those moments when, graciously and unexpectedly, my dried-up heart recovers greenness. And "The Easter" is the Big Event, the resurrection from the dead, the life everlasting. "All things are yours . . . whether . . . the world, or life, or death, or things present, or things to come; all are yours; and ye are Christ's, and Christ is God's" (1 Corinthians 3:21–23).

ᴥᔓ | What Do You Mean—Pay Attention?

What is it like to pay attention?
Is it parting forests with your fingers tree by tree?
Is it listening hard to grass?
Is it framing sunlight in smaller and smaller windows?
Is it standing dead still in the middle of the town?
Is it floating blindfold on the sea?
Is it looking through the sidewalk to the middle
    of the earth?
Is it sitting upright in the sky?
Is it flying backwards?
Is it flying forwards?
Is it flying over continents?
Is it flying into space?
Is it eye-screwing the black point on the
    white wall through to the other side?
Is it staying awake all night?
Is it forgetting and forgetting?
Is it always staying half asleep?
Is it remembering and remembering?
Is it breathing with everybody else's lungs?
Is it opening out your bones?
Is it holding your breath forever?
None of these.

MEDITATION

Paying attention is so completely simple and obvious. Or is it? We tell our children, "Pay attention!" and we fully expect a five-year-old to know exactly what we mean. But the actual *doing* of it—that's something else again! In a memorable passage from one of his sermons, John Donne described how he would try to concentrate by entering into his closet to pray. But when God and all the holy angels had responded to his invitation to commune in prayer, the mere sound of a coach on the road outside, or even the buzzing of a fly, would be enough to distract his attention.

Anybody who has ever tried to pray will recognize the problem. If it isn't an external distraction—a car screeching its brakes, the jangle of the telephone—it's an internal distraction, the incessant egobabble. Yet Simone Weil and many other mystics have pointed out that the discipline of paying attention is the without-which-nothing, the absolute bottom-line of experiencing oneness with God.

So Catherine asks, "What is it like to pay attention?" Apparently it has something to do with being totally absorbed in what we are doing, so absorbed we lose all consciousness of ourselves as separate beings. Perhaps it is like counting the trees in the forest, being careful not to forget the tally yet equally careful not to miss one of the trees? Or listening to the growing of the grass, with our whole being concentrated in the ear so as not to miss the most elusive sound? Or imagining the gradual focus of sunlight in smaller and smaller patches as the field of concentration narrows? Or standing utterly still in the middle óf all the busyness of life? Or floating blindfolded in the ocean, with all our senses concentrated on the rocking motion in which we are immersed? Or looking at a crack in the sidewalk so intently that it suddenly seems to go clear into the heart of the earth? Or sitting upright in the sky, the soul simultaneously alert to the vertical and horizontal dimensions? Or flying backward to the anterior life—becoming as unconscious of time and space as we were before we were born? Or flying forward to future life, becoming as unconscious of space and time as we may be in eternity? Or watching out the jet plane window as whole continents pass beneath us far below? Or being propelled into space by a great rocket? Or staring so closely at a black point on a white background that we feel as if we have emerged on the other side? Or staying awake instead of sleeping, never letting the exterior life gain any importance whatsoever? Or constantly forgetting the exterior life? or staying only *half* asleep, always open to images that float up from the unconscious mind, attending to the exterior life yet never giving ourselves over to it completely? Or constantly reminding ourselves of the true nature of Reality? Or so completely empathizing with other people that we lose any sense of our own lungs and seem to be breathing with theirs? Or stripping flesh off our bones by complete self-revelation and utter transparency? Or being able to hold our breath not only until we can think of nothing else, but everlastingly?

Are these what it is like to pay attention?

No. Paying attention is like none of these, says Catherine. It is like none of these because while it may be like any of these sometimes, it is like none of these all the time. It is both less than these and more than these. It is nameless, just as its effects are nameless. Although we can discipline our minds with academic studies, artistic practice, and the like, we cannot achieve the ability to pay ultimate attention simply on demand. Like all aspects of the spiritual life, paying attention is paradoxical. We rest in grace, yet we are anxious to grow, to love God more perfectly, to *see* what we are looking at.

Paying attention is active—and passive. It is an achievement—and it is a gift.

✑ | Dusty Fun

> God laughs and plays.
> —*Meister Eckhart*

Dry mouth, dry eye, dry day—
Like monks planting sticks
For God panache,
Not flowers.

MEDITATION

Meister Eckhart envisions a God who laughs and plays. But sometimes we human beings experience times that are anything but playful—days when we could swear that the ultimate proof of our existence is simply the fact of our anguish. "I suffer, therefore I am." At such times the thought of a laughing, playing God can seem very offensive.

Catherine asks herself, how do my times of misery relate to the laughter of God? In response, she remembers a medieval legend in which some monks were asked to plant sticks as a sign of their obedience. Whereas no external flowers would ever come of this planting, nevertheless there was the invisible beauty of the gardeners' motivation, their desire to serve God utterly. For the laughing God, those sticks would be as ornamental, as full of verve and flamboyance, as the most gorgeous of plantings.

Similarly, our dryness may well become God's crown of flowers if we are willing to "tough it out" in faithful yieldedness to a will much larger than our own comprehension of it. The fact is that we are exceedingly confused about our own best interests anyhow. As long as we wish to be open to God's will, we might just as well begin by accepting the misery of the moment and the thought that maybe, just maybe, God is laughing at us.

St. Paul says that "the sufferings of this present time are not worthy to be compared with the glory which shall be revealed in us"(Romans 8:18). And when we read about the sufferings of other people, it seems easy enough to believe that their sufferings will be transformed into glory. Their sufferings seem so solid, so valid. But our own—our own seem so ordinary, so induced by our own flawed perceptions. How can they result in glory? Yet even pangs like these are the dry sticks which we must plant for God's panache.

No doubt if we had God's vision of the glory that shall follow, we'd be laughing too.

ᴥᔑ | *Mors, Amor*

Love I remember all the time,
But as for being dead—that, only twice.
Once I was three and ill;
I saw from my bed
Some moving clouds
And thought how they would carry me away,
Though it was very young to die.
And I remember later
How my father lay
One Sunday afternoon
On a couch in a cloud of music
From New York or somewhere,
And I thought—
Well, we shall die together now.
Yet, as today I speak,
He is twenty-nine years really dead,
And I a hundred two still here.
I've survived so long,
I cannot tell how many
Worms have turned
Since I've even thought of clouds,
But love I remember all the time.

MEDITATION

Love and death are two of the inescapable components of human experience. Because they are so central to the human condition, we may image and conceptualize them differently at different stages of our lives.

Catherine remembers a time when as a child she thought of dying as being wafted away on a cloud into the sky. She also remembers another time, in her adolescence, when she and her father were surrounded by a cloud of music on a Sunday afternoon. She felt such perfect identification with her father at that blissful moment that life seemed utterly fulfilled. Dreamily she embraced the thought of death's arrival in the very perfection of life.

But now that she is middle-aged, her father has been dead for over twenty-nine years. He is really dead, not caught up in some cloudy illusion. And his death and those twenty-nine intervening years have left Catherine feeling ancient, perhaps a hundred and two, and certainly with a much more hard-headed perspective on what it means to die. The reference to worms assures us of that in several ways: by reminding us of corruption in the grave and by causing us to think of the thousand miniscule humiliations a shy person may endure before the worm turns. These little deaths can make life seem long and even the grave seem less repulsive. One thing is sure: in middle age one rarely thinks in terms of cloudy and romantic love-deaths.

So much for death. But what about love?

Catherine begins and ends with exactly the same statement: "love I remember all the time." Thus love brings the poem full circle, as it brings a grace-filled life full circle. A person who is welcomed into the world by loving parents receives a lifelong legacy of love. The assurance of being loved and loveable is always there in the veins, functioning as unconsciously and life-supportively as the pumping of the blood. Catherine was fortunate enough to have received this priceless legacy, and despite the changes in her perception of life and death, love continues to function "all the time."

On another level, however, the first and final lines speak for the experience not only of Catherine but of every human being, whether or not our infancy was imbued with the love of our parents. Acts 17:28 tells us that God "is not far from every one of us," for in God "we live and move and have our being." This is an image of all humanity's being nurtured and carried in the gigantic womb of God the Mother-Father Almighty. No matter how vague, it is the fact of this irrevocable relationship to the Creator that is the light that enlightens every person who is born into this world (John 1:9). Because we have forgotten our Origin, we must be brought back to God through belief in the true Light; but the darkness has never been able to engulf it completely (John 1:5). Thus, either through a deeply unconscious encoding that the darkness cannot erase, or through the joyous conscious acceptance of the believer, "love [we] remember all the time."

◄§ | A Cosmology in Three Parts for Three Persons

I.

Child women
At the center of Paradise,
We split egg rolls
In a primeval forest
Full of calico cat eyes,
Strew bowls of milk at the edge of oceans,
Share sun lotion across planed mountains
Falling into the sea.
Endless joy in a cosmos in reverse.

II.

I am lost
Have lost my footing in slithering space,
Am falling
From cracked floor to floor,
From pit to fissured pit
Into your heart's exploding fault.

III.

My private, secret clown
Grinning in the air,
Tumbling in the spheres,
You force me to joy
At our parallel propulsions
That never meet.
You are right: we will take tightrope walks together
In heaven's heaven,
But it will never, never be made plain.

MEDITATION

Relationships are of primary importance during the spiritual journey. Rather than cultivating one-dimensional religious warmth without concern for the whole person, genuinely spiritual people seek to form fully human relationships. Catherine calls this poem a "cosmology" in order to indicate that being-in-community constitutes the whole world for her. She believes that relationships form the prism through which any individual must view the universe. Accordingly she describes three very significant relationships in her life. And, since honestly described individual experience often turns out to be universal, the three relationships prove to be types that most of the rest of us are familiar with.

Part One describes a friendship in which Catherine feels completely secure, open, and easy. Because she and her friend share a mystical view of life, a view that reverses the world's usual competitive values, the two of them are "child women." Their faith in God and each other makes the crooked straight and the rough places plain; so they happily share sun lotion across planed mountains at the center of Paradise. Although tremendous things are happening in the world, they find their joy in little things. They are still. They are centered. Some of us are fortunate enough to know at least one person with whom our identification is so strong, and our understanding so intuitive, that we are utterly at ease in their presence.

But the "easy" relationship is not the only kind. Part Two describes a relationship of terrific complexity, insecurity, and danger. In Catherine's case this was a person met in mid-life, bringing a totally unexpected friendship, catapulating her into whole new currents of thought, and at the same time stirring feelings that had lain dormant for years. Such relationships can be liberating, refreshing, and terrifying all at the same time. If Part One describes the ease of intuitive identity ("my own soul in another body"), Part Two describes the challenge of *otherness* ("Who is this person? who am I in relationship to such a person? what do I owe to this person?") Our lives are poor indeed without this kind of challenge.

Part Three describes a relationship in which sameness and otherness are balanced in a kind of polarity. This is a relationship with a spiritual counterpart of the other sex. The two of them experience the tensions of gender-differences (taking tightrope walks together) and experience life from completely parallel points of view that never quite fuse and never will fuse, not even in the joyous eternity they expect to share. Whereas the first relationship is so easy that even mountains are planed down to the ordinary dimensions of sun lotion, this one is so *other* despite its similar direction that its essence will "never, never, be made plain." And whereas the second relationship is volcanic in its nearly total otherness, this one involves the full acceptance of spiritual unity despite differentness and mystery.

Identity, otherness, parallelism-without-fusion .... Security, danger, living-with-complexity.... Ease, opposition, joy-in-diversity.... Such varied relationships do indeed form an orderly system, a cosmology.

◄§ | Conversation During
a Summer Solstice

I believe only in appearances
And in the inaccessible.
I believe only in your total presence
And your total absence.

I don't have to tell you
The fire will fire
The light light
The void void
And our laugh laugh last.

MEDITATION

There is a kind of internal conversation that some people would call prayer. Catherine does not call this poem "Prayer During a Summer Solstice" because there are so many other kinds of prayer: silent recollection, for instance, or structured meditation, or simple gratitude, or intercession, or liturgy. But she would not deny that this conversation is with God.

In a sense, the conversation is a mini-credo: "I believe only in appearances/ And in the inaccessible." What Catherine does *not* believe in are abstractions, clichés, theories, categorizations, preachments, platitudes, and the like. Having reverence for things as they are, she believes in nature (ordinary external reality) and in supernature (a largely elusive interior and transcendent reality). She believes in God's presence (being and becoming) and in God's absence (nothingness).

She realizes, of course, the rich irony that it is she and not the Person to whom she speaks who *needs* this conversation. It is she (the speaker) who often gets upset at her lack of control over life, who forgets that nature quietly took its course before her birth and will continue to do so not only after her physical death, but during all the phases of life when she is in no condition to imagine that she is "helping things along." The fire continues to flame (be fire), the light continues to give forth its light, emptiness continues to empty out its own emptiness. And for this very reason—the continuity and reliability of being and nothingness—creature and Creator can laugh together in the sheer joy of Being.

The summer solstice is, of course, a culmination-point, the longest day of the year. One could even view it as a pivot point that centers the remainder of the year whirling around it. As such, the solstice nicely symbolizes the profound center of all being, the still point upon which the world turns. It is only from the stance of the still point of connection with God, involving utter trust in the Structure and Process of Reality, that any human being can feel confident of having the last laugh.

Keeping a quiet heart about ultimate well-being is especially important for those of us who are activists or workaholics. Because injustice is so excruciating, we who try to bring about progress toward God's earthly reign of peace and justice sometimes tend to forget that the salvation of the world does not depend on us alone. For the standpoint of the Eternal Now, salvation is already accomplished. This remembrance is not intended to squelch our efforts toward social justice, but rather to clarify the perspective from which we work. We can keep our energies flowing cleanly and sweetly—we can avoid burn-out—by reminding ourselves that at "the still point of the turning world," everything is all right, everything is perfected.

At the end of Geoffrey Chaucer's masterpiece, *Troilus and Criseyde*, Troilus is killed in battle and is carried up to the eighth sphere in the heavens. From this vantage point he looks down at the anguish of those who weep over his death and remembers his life on earth—the torment of losing Criseyde's love, the lonely sufferings of battle. Aware of all the energy he had invested in his torment, Troilus throws back his head and . . . *laughs!*

When we laugh from a similar vantage point, we will not be mocking what we have endured, nor negating it. We will be relieved, heart-happy, to realize that what seemed deadly important is not so significant after all, and that everything truly important has been brought to fruition. The fire continues to flame, the light is lit, nothingness negates nothingness, and together with God, we laugh the last laugh.

◆§ | *Memoria involuntaria*

I have been riding the talgo since the Renaissance.
The Escorial comes always without warning
Rising on the dry right with floating flute and guitar.
And Juan of Fontiveros comes over and over
Up and down the aisle
Serving wine, cheese, and himself.

It could be dead summer or December in America.
Above my house the geese derailed from seasons
Whistle without warning that the train goes on,
    no matter.
I have heard the shape of court notes without warning
So many times since Spain
That I know the talgo rides on in sweet sleep
Behind my veiled bones.

MEDITATION

The title of this poem is in Spanish because the poem itself transposes an actual train trip Catherine took through Spain in 1968.
The phrase "involuntary memory" is adapted from Marcel Proust's
"mémoire involontaire," by which Proust means those memories
that return unbidden and which Proust wants to preserve forever
through an act of creative intelligence such as making a painting,
poem, or statue, or, in his case, writing a scene in a novel. The
point is that whereas these memories can be "frozen" forever

through artistic effort, no amount of intellectual effort will force the memories to return until they do so unaccountably. They are thus involuntary.

For Catherine, the ride on the *talgo* (a high-class Spanish train) has provided not only an involuntary memory which she preserves in this poem, but something even more than Proust intended by his phrase. On that train ride, Catherine experienced such delight that she was catapulted clean out of ordinary time and space and into another dimension that seems to return to some degree every time she remembers the train. Hence, she has been riding that *talgo* "since the Renaissance." As she sits in her suburban home writing about her experience in a Spanish train, she hears Canadian geese overhead, realizes that it is not the usual season to hear them (they are "derailed from seasons"), and is reminded by the whistle of their wings that the *talgo*-ride is eternal (that is, also "derailed from seasons") now that it has become a part of her eternal consciousness.

While the train was passing through the arid hills of northern Spain (the homeland of John of the Cross, the famous mystic who was born in Fontiveros), the train's loudspeakers had been playing courtly flute and guitar music. Now, unexpectedly, while she is engrossed in something else, Catherine will suddenly hear "the shape of [those] court notes without warning." At such times the music calls up the whole world she has associated with it. Thus she knows that the whole experience on the *talgo* is constantly within her, sometimes quiescent ("in sweet sleep"), sometimes active, but always there inside.

During that 1968 train ride, Catherine had sat watching the dry Spanish hills, hearing the flute and guitar, and thinking about communion with God as described by St. John of the Cross (Juan of Fontiveros). Suddenly, off to the right of the train amidst the dryness, she saw the splendid vast Renaissance palace known as the Escorial. Not expecting to see any such thing, she was astonished. And now, whenever something brings back the involuntary memory of the train ride, it comes complete with the astonishment of finding a magnificent palace right in the middle of an arid countryside.

St. Augustine speaks about "the shine of the reason," the enlightenment that is always present within twice-born human beings, but which manifests itself only on certain (often unexpected) occasions. English poet William Wordsworth speaks of "spots of time," moments of experience that when recalled have a positive moral and spiritual effect on him. Whether we call them by Proust's *"mémoire involontaire,"* Augustine's "shine of reason," or Wordsworth's "spots of time," most of us have our own equivalent of Catherine's experience in the Spanish train. Like hers, these memories have resurfaced so often that we know they are continually within us, riding on "in sweet sleep/ Behind [our] veiled bones."

◄§ | February

In cold months
The truest illusion
Is to trick the wind
By seeming numb

If all doors are fast,
Save your strength
For picking locks
Or slipping messages underneath
To warm fires playing dumb.

MEDITATION

For many of us, February is the cruelest month of the year. The rejuvenation of Spring seems a weary long way ahead. The glorious show of Fall has dwindled long since to a bleakness, and the snow has long ago worn out its welcome. February and the other cold months speak to us of those times when life seems almost unliveable because God, warmth, and pleasure seem to have withdrawn from us completely. How are we to muscle through such times?

Catherine suggests that the best plan is to find whatever route to comfort and survival is at hand, even if it is nothing more satisfactory than pretending to be numb to the chill blasts of the wind. If the doors are locked, don't try to force them; instead, delicately and gently pick the locks, going according to your own nature instead of trying to run roughshod over it. For instance, it might be better to read a good book or clean the house or take a walk in the woods than to try to pray at such a time. If you discover you cannot pick the locks, then slip messages underneath the door to communicate with the warm fires inside. In other words, despite the fact that you are getting no response from your inner being and hence are left "out in the cold," continue to act as if all is well. Do what you would have done anyway, assuming that truth and love are still warm inside you even though you cannot actually feel their presence.

The warm fires are in truth still burning, even though they are behind locked doors, and you will be more comfortable if you will cajole yourself by pretending to be in contact with them all along. If God is playing a little trick on you by pretending to be absent, play a little trick in return by pretending to be in communion. This illusion will actually be more true to reality than succumbing to despair by accepting coldness as the final reality. The warmth will come again, the life will stir. Your world will not be winter-locked forever. Take for your own heart the comfort Percy Shelley spoke to his: "If winter comes, can spring be far behind?" The fires remain warm after all; and they are only *playing* dumb.

⁌ | The Supper

The supper that enkindles love
Works wonders too with flesh and blood.
The supper stirs your hand
And I see the five capes of that calm continent
Circle in from the sea around the plum.
Excess of time-stop exceeds time, I suppose,
Or else, your hand around the plum
      is the only time.

MEDITATION

A supper is less formal than a dinner. Whereas a dinner may be a grand occasion with many guests, supper sounds more friendly and intimate. So it is especially lovely that during one of the mystical experiences described by St. John of the Cross, Christ invited John to sit down to supper with Him. That was a "supper that enkindle[d] love," just as the Eucharist or Communion, re-enacting the Last Supper, is a "supper that enkindles love."

But Catherine suggests that the transfiguration of life that occurs during a mystical experience or during the Eucharist can also do wonders during an ordinary meal with friends. Getting more specific, she describes watching a friend's hand close around a plum. The five fingers ("capes") of the hand ("that calm continent") "circle in from the sea" of eternity in two senses: that all persons are eternal, and that this hand belongs to a person who is aware of being a "partaker of the divine nature" (2 Peter 1:4). But at this moment the friend circles his firm hand firmly around a firm plum.

Watching this simple act, Catherine thinks about the nature of reality. That hand around that plum seems somehow *ultimate*. Time seems to stop, to put an end to time, to create eternity. What happens at such moments? Perhaps the sense of time's stoppage exceeds time, so that time is simply transformed into no-time (that is, into eternity). Or perhaps the hand around the plum *is* eternal reality—is and always has been the only time there is, with chronological time being the sheer delusion.

But, after all, what does it matter? By whatever method, the supper with a friend has put us in touch with What Is Real. Working wonders with flesh and food, the supper has enkindled love.

↝ | Lemonade

The path of lemons
Winds back through summers
To the first time I sat on the porch at night
And offered pale lemon rain
My mother made
To the cool night sky lemon shifting.

It is lemon time again—
In a way New Jersey summers
Are no newer than New England's—
But I draw the knife down now
In my own kitchen on yellow victims
Spurting tears more tart than then,
And I drink my potion in the day
To the hot sky god
That's very still.

MEDITATION

The contrast in this poem is between a girl's drinking the lemonade prepared for her by her mother, and the same girl years later,
now-become-woman, drinking lemonade prepared by herself in
her own kitchen. Any object can of course lead us back to other
places and other times and to the contrasts that reward us with insight about ourselves. In this case, the pathway to insight is paved
with lemons.

Childhood lemonade was nocturnal, associated with coolness and with a pale lemon-colored moon in its shifting variety. All is flexible, open, vacillating, irresponsible, dependent yet dynamic. By contrast, adult lemonade is diurnal, associated with the hot sun standing still in a dry sky. All is stable, tense, well-lit, cruelly responsible, deathlike, and centered.

Catherine pictures herself as a witch executing her yellow victims whose tears are needed to form her poison-potion (the lemonade). There is a great deal of pain involved in breaking away from childhood dependence on mother and becoming one's own person. Maturity and independence are costly.

Part of the cost is that adulthood forces upon us the unwelcome realization that somebody always has to pay a price for our pleasure. Although lemonade seems in childhood as natural and free as the rain, in adulthood there is no lemonade without going to the trouble of making it or buying it. Either way, it entails the sacrifice of the lemons.

The summers in New Jersey, where Catherine's adult home is located, are really not any "newer" than summers in New England, where Catherine grew up, because summers spell lemonade in either place. But it does not therefore follow that lemonade is lemonade is lemonade. If lemonade has really *always* been the tears of the lemon rather than pure lemon rain, nevertheless to the adult awareness, the taste is more tart than it seemed in simpler days. But of course there is no returning to childhood or to the perceptions of childhood.

One thing, however, remains constant. In childhood Catherine offered her lemonade to a cool night sky; in adulthood, she drinks to a hot sky god. What is constant is the sense of relationship to the world, however differently that world may be perceived as the summers come and pass and then return again. That relationship to overarching reality is after all what provides life with its "redeeming social value," its center and its meaning.

Dear Meister Eckhart

In this school of the dead,
Lessons are dead simple:
Classes are often in the air
Or sometimes anywhere downtown.

If we ever get a thought,
The white wool ghost disappears
Behind his finger and his voice:
"If that is what you think,
You're on the wrong track."

Homework is reducing numbers
To a little less than nothing;
Calisthenics?—tossing ourselves
Off both ends of the chain—
And the slow are sent forever
Sweeping up the floor.

But some days he is so white and light,
He cannot help himself,
And he skips around the room
Joking with his dunces
About the fun of God.

MEDITATION

In this poem Catherine imagines Eckhart teaching school. It would have to be a school "of the dead" for several reasons: because Eckhart himself has been dead for centuries, because Eckhart when alive was dead to his old nature and alive unto Christ, and because anyone who wants to understand Eckhart must be willing to die to private ego-concerns in order to live life more abundantly. The classes are "dead simple" because they simply require death. They ask human beings to simplify their lives by conforming their wills to that of the One Love which (as Dante put it)"drives the sun and the other stars."

Classes are often "in the air" because at times Eckhart can sound quite abstruse. On the other hand, classes are "Sometimes anywhere downtown" because Eckhart is frequently quite down to earth. And it doesn't really matter where you are, since connection with God can be established anyplace as long as it is right here and right now.

Catherine refers to Eckhart as a "white wool ghost" because his habit as a Dominican priest was made of white wool. He disappears into scolding and disapproving whenever his students begin to theorize and conceptualize about God. No concepts or theological arguments will provide authentic contact with God, who lives in the cloud of unknowing and can be reached only through honest desire.

For homework, Eckhart assigns his students to free ourselves from the notion of multiplicity, which is one of the barriers that keep us from coming to God. We must learn by experience that the multiplicity of appearances ultimately disappears into the oneness of reality.

As for calisthenics, we are assigned to the difficult task of tossing ourselves off both ends of a chain. In theology, all profound truth is paradoxical or perhaps dialectical. Apparent contrasts turn out upon deeper reflection to be unified—contrasts such as exterior and interior, knowledge and love, the accessible appearance and the inaccessible reality, and so forth. It was Pascal who utilized an image of a chain on which both ends are infinite. If the ends of that chain are ever to meet, it must be only in infinity. So Eckhart's students must learn the discipline of jumping off *both* ends of the chain, having the truth and yet never having it, all at the same time.

As for those who cannot quite comprehend such things, Eckhart suggests that we classify ourselves as beginners among beginners. There is always a need for someone to sweep the floor!

But some days our teacher Eckhart is so full of divine hilarity that he cannot help skipping around the classroom, joking with us students about the light-hearted capers of God. For there is in Eckhart—and in the awareness of most of those who claim to have had direct contact with God—a strong appreciation of God's sense of humor.

It was Eckhart who told us that "the eye with which I see God is the same eye with which God sees me." Fortunately for us all, there is an amused twinkle in that eye.

ꝏ | Bad Weather

I will say what little
I have breath to say—
Utter rain and utter bone,
Pain of damp and limping love,
Pain of too little patience and too little cry,
And at the day's end,
Pity of streetlights parting the sky
Enough to squeeze a thumbnail through.
See, you will not be rid of me this soon.

MEDITATION

No matter how spiritual we may be or may yearn to be, we remain human and are affected by such things as bad weather. Compassion and love are the human essence, but on some days we feel we have very little of either to give. What we have plenty of at such times are aggression and hostility. Our love is damp and limping, and we feel pained by that fact. We feel pained also by our lack of patience with ourselves and other people; and yet we have too little strength or energy to cry out to God for help. What to do? Nothing. Nothing to do but wait.

Finally, hope begins to revive. The return of hope is like the lighting of streetlights at evening. The beauty of them seems to open up the sky for us—only to the width of a fingernail, to be sure, but even that little suggestion of hope is enough. Our weary souls are stirred by life's beauty just enough to start over again in their search for God and godliness. There is even a hint of begrudging amusement as we pick ourselves up and say to God, "See, you will not be rid of me this soon!" As William Faulkner said, it is of the essence of our humanity that we *endure.*

St. Catherine of Sienna once wrote that it is possible to suffer without pain. The seat of all pain, she said, is in the will. As long as our will is willing only what God wills, there is no pain even in the suffering we may be called upon to endure. Such a statement can probably never be understood by a person who has never had the experience of loss, bereavement, or other deprivation while being constantly bouyed up by a sense of God's loving purpose and presence. That is what suffering without pain is all about. It is possible; it is a reality; but it must be experienced to be believed.

For most of us, suffering ticks off instant rebellion. ("Why me? What did I ever do to deserve this?") And this recoil against reality is the root of our pain. The pain can be minimized and perhaps even dissolved by leaning into the suffering, by relaxation, by acceptance of reality. And that goes for "small things" like bad weather and our sense of deficiency in patience, love, and strength. Simply waiting—suffering without trying to crush, destroy, or deny our suffering—may be the wisest course of action after all. For at the end of the experience, the streetlights will come on, compassion will reawaken, strength will return.

We might as well learn to let go and let be. . . . Because with or without our pain, everything is going to turn out all right.

❦ | Work and Play

Working that hard
  is like a rage
    that one is helpless
      before Energy
        in stable light.
It is as hard not to work
  as to work with geometry and finesse.
I am worn to the bone
Trying to play
        trying not to play,
And trying not to play
        trying to play.

MEDITATION

Many young people seem to care very little about work. Perhaps their carelessness stems from observing the workaholic obsessions of some of us who are older. For centuries, in fact, hard work has been viewed almost as an end in itself. If cleanliness was next to godliness, hard work was the means of achieving them both.

People who were brought up in a workaholic culture tend to view spiritual growth also as a matter of hard work. We worked at learning to pray; we worked at discerning the will of God; we worked at proper behavior. Catherine identifies the tendency to overwork as a symptom of anger at God—anger that we feel helpless in the face of God's ability to be still and simultaneously to be the dynamic source of all energy. We want to deny our helplessness

before destiny, so we try to hide our helplessness even from ourselves by sheer busyness.

Because we are so frequently out of harmony with Ultimate
Energy, we also have to work hard at overcoming our obsession
with achievement. We even work hard at playing! We feel trapped
between our own inability to stop working and our inability to
work well—that is, with the proper combination of science and
artistry, precision and perfection, geometry and finesse. The nearly
impossible feat for most of us is to work well: harmoniously, with
single focus, perfectly absorbed, unconscious of ourselves. Because
working well is so difficult, most of us spend most of our time
either overworking or working distractedly.

Working well—flowing smoothly with the flow of All That Is—
restores energy even while it utilizes energy. The flow of energy
goes two ways in all work that is properly accomplished; that is,
the worker feels restored, is a receiver as well as a giver. But self-
conscious attempts to stop working, like inauthentic working, are
both exhausting and enervating. Catherine symbolizes all this by
concluding her poem with a statement that is deliberately absurd
and painfully self-conscious. "I am worn to the bone," the speaker
confesses, with my efforts to concentrate on concentration (trying
to play at not playing) and with trying not to be conscious of unself-
consciousness (trying not to play trying to play). Like a dog chasing
its tail, self-consciousness makes graceful living impossible. We trip
ourselves all over the place.

What is the solution to our dilemma? Surrender to Reality. Drop-
ping our counterproductive rage at being helpless before "Energy/
in stable light." Accepting God's gift of grace. Letting go of self-
consciousness. Letting God do our work through us. In a state of
grace, work seems effortless—in fact, it seems like play.

❧ | The Four Elements

I pulled the tip of my finger
Out of the keyhole,
And you came in, my ghost,
Bringing so much bouillabaisse
Smelled from the upper room
But left downstairs unsipped.

We lifted the ladle a million times,
Till gasping for thirst and air,
I opened the window and released the sea
Tapping and taunting on the panes.

It came in full flood on you and me
Now merged to a bloated boat
Filled with fluid fish,
And we launched into a thirsty sea
Of two times a million two of a kind
Sea creatures quite as drunk as we.

In forty days and forty nights
We and the waters tired
And collapsed into a small fire bird
Tapping and taunting on dry mountain ground.

MEDITATION

In pre-Socratic philosophy, and indeed throughout the Middle Ages and the Renaissance, the created universe was thought to consist of just four elements: air, water, fire, and earth. Catherine structures her poem around these four elements, focusing most of the poem on water (associated with the womb and the unconscious mind). She comes to the fire, air, and earth only in the final two lines.

The keyhole is a common psychoanalytic symbol for getting clues from our unconscious mind. To block or stuff the keyhole is therefore to resist insight and growth. When Catherine speaks of taking the tip of her finger out of the keyhole, she symbolizes the relaxation of her guard against unconscious images and attitudes. No sooner has she let down her guard than in comes "My ghost," meaning her past and the images built up in her unconscious mind. Her ghost carries with it some self-awareness (the bouillabaisse, a large fish stew) which she has intuited ("smelled") within her conscious mind ("the upper room") but has not really allowed herself to experience consciously. Prior to this time, that is, she has been leaving a great deal of stuff unexamined in the depths of unconsciousness ("downstairs unsipped").

Together, her body and spirit examine the content of her memories and experiences ("we lift the ladle a million times") until finally she feels so overwhelmed that she permits the inrush of the entire ocean of her unconsciousness to flood in upon her ("opened the window and released the sea"). All the things that had peripherally teased her consciousness ("tapping and taunting on the pane") are now admitted to fuller awareness.

The sensation is, to say the least, uncomfortable. The images in stanza three capture the discomfort, the expansiveness, and the heady danger of evolving through confrontation with all the stuff that was formerly unconscious. The sea, the fish, the boat, and the Self merge into oneness as the consciousness makes conquest of the mind's previously unexplored depths. This is the inward journey which each of us must undertake before we are ready and able to explore external reality with any objectivity.

Dr. Elisabeth Kübler-Ross says that the reason we are not able to hear what the dying are trying to tell us is that we ourselves are full of unconfronted fears and neuroses. We must finish our own "unfinished business," she counsels, laying to rest our own ghosts, before we can be free to hear accurately what other people are trying to say to us.

The image of the undifferentiated sea of consciousness/unconsciousness/body/spirit/world/self now merges into the image of Noah's flood. After "forty days and forty nights"—the time period associated in the Bible with spiritual preparation, self-knowledge, and transformation—the whole watery self-exploration experience is transformed into a phoenix, "a small fire bird/ Tapping and taunting on the dry mountain ground." The phoenix, or fire bird, is a famous symbol of death and resurrection, since it periodically immolates itself and then is reborn out of its own ashes, rising into the air of new life. Just as the contents of the unconscious mind had teased and flirted with consciousness, now the dead-and-resurrected Self will tease and flirt with external reality, seeking to find better revelations in the solid creation and in the "dry mountain ground" of Mt. Ararat, the mountain of spiritual ascent.

Having completed the watery journey inward (the journey of self-understanding), the Self is now on solid ground, fulfilled by a successful harmony between consciousness and unconsciousness. The result is freedom from navel-gazing and a movement from passivity to activity in the "objective" world. The one who was tapped and taunted now does the tapping and taunting. After the journey inward come the freedom and the energy for the journey out. After the water come the fire, and the air, and the earth.

৵ | Jones Beach, A Sunday in November

Just because eye has not seen
Is no alibi for never peeking.
Because ear has not heard
Is no excuse for not eavesdropping.
There are days like today
To gull-flip a double passport
At the border of small infinities
And stare at shells
That talk out loud.

MEDITATION

"Eye hath not seen, nor ear heard, neither have entered in the heart
of . . . [humankind], the things which God hath prepared for them
that love . . . [God]" (1 Corinthians 2:9). Thus St. Paul quotes
from the prophet Isaiah (64:4). So we have the witness of both
Hebrew and Christian Scriptures that God's provision for God's
children is beyond anything we have seen, or heard, or even can
imagine.

Still, it's fun to try. Like children confident of their mother's
indulgence, we can peek excitedly through the bannister on Christmas morning. Like children trusting in their father's love, we can
strain our ears to catch a few phrases of late-night plans for tomor-
row's outing.

Take, for instance, a visit to Jones Beach one Sunday in Novem-
ber. On such a visit, we can let ourselves become one spirit with a
free-wheeling gull, flipping one single passport that admits us

both to earth and sky, time and eternity. Circling gracefully above the beach within the flesh and feathers of the gull, we gaze down at the seashells below. Eavesdropping, we hear them speak of their Creator.

Many of us interpret the meaning of "loving God" in a very narrow fashion, as if the point were for all of us to focus our love upon a single person who hogs the limelight the way a rock star is made the focus of a million passions during a concert. Catherine's point here is very different: that to love any aspect of reality is to love God, who is the Being behind all being, the Person behind all personhood, the Structure and Process and Energizer of all that is. We can have no idea of what it will be like to see God face to face without delusions or distortions. But that's "no alibi for never peeking." We can in the meantime love God through appreciative enjoyment of all that God has made.

"Hier ist die sägliche Zeit, hier seine Heimat"—Rilke

No one should wait too long to speak.
Yet, too early speaking in cages of our own invention
Is not to have understood the true zoo of childhood dreams.
In any case, wiring the word for sound
Is not so different from amplifying echo:
Frail notes twist to fine tornadoes
In the living rooms and attics of our clones.
If not that, our words are spirited to some other space
Beyond the listeners' surmise.
It is always too late and too early to speak
By any measure that we understand,
Except that here is the saying's time
And here the word is home.

MEDITATION

Is it better to be silent than to speak? Communication is deceptively
difficult. Is it even possible, ever, to get someone else to perceive
precisely the message we are trying to send? How can a clear message be received by faulty receivers when even the sending set is
faulty? Many times we feel like Eliot's Prufrock, who lamented
that it was impossible to say exactly what he meant. Or like lesser
versions of William Faulkner who admitted that his reason for
starting a new novel was always that he had not quite managed to
say what he meant to say in the last one.

The more profound our vision of immeasurable reality, the more frustrating is the attempt to put it into words. For that reason, despite the thousands of eloquent attempts through the centuries to articulate what really happened, experiences of direct communion with God are properly described as ineffable. Beyond words. Whatever we have to say about the Godhead, He/She/It is more than that, different from that, but never precisely that.

And yet, if we do not attempt now to communicate the mysteries that have been revealed to us, when will we ever speak? As German poet Rainer Maria Rilke wrote, "here—[in this life, in this world] —here is the saying's time,/ And here the word is home." For that reason, despite the frustrations of trying to communicate, "No one should wait too long to speak."

Speech or silence: like every other ultimate question, this one resolves only by means of paradox. The night cometh, when no person will be able to speak—so the time is now. And yet, to speak too soon is to reduce reality to a premature theory, a straitjacket, a "cage of our own invention." To speak too soon is to violate the complexity of genuine intuitive vision ("the true zoo of childhood dreams"). To speak too soon is to speak with undeveloped awareness, inauthentically, without creativity.

The Christian theological justification for all words is of course Jesus the Word. That Word is always home (simultaneously *our* home and *at* home). It is our obligation to express that Word. . . . But it must be expressed out of silence, with full awareness that nothing we can say will ever do justice to the Way, the Truth, and the Life.

After he had finished his stupendous systematic theology, St. Thomas Aquinas experienced a direct vision of God. In response he fell silent and laid down his pen forever, with the single exclamation that "Everything is straw." Similarly, when Job, who by God's own admission had spoken truly about God, was directly confronted by God out of the whirlwind, he cried out, "I have spoken of great things which I have not understood, things too wonderful for me to know. I knew of thee only by report, but now I see thee with my own eyes. Therefore I melt away; I repent in dust and ashes" (Job 42:3–6, NEB).

For all these reasons, "It is always too late and too early to speak/ By any measure that we understand." And yet, when our deepest nature prompts us to break silence, speak we must!

⤙ | Leaving

I waited
But I could not wait.
And I knew I was the lamed palfrey
Turning into a horse on the trot
Across the field
Today turned white with winter,
Leaving a trail of one small hoof
Pressed deeper than the rest,
Staying one moment longer.
But now the leaving's done,
Who can tell there was a horse?
Who would know rider from the ground,
Or snow from the light on it?

MEDITATION

Do I dare to believe that despite all my faults, I am admitted into
the friendship of God? How do I gain the courage to step out and
act upon the faith that my ego-nature has been crucified "with all
its affections and lusts"? That I really am created anew in Christ
Jesus, the New Humanity? It seems too *arrogant* to believe that
Christ lives in me. (In the apostles Peter and Paul, yes, of course;
but in *me*?)

Many of us experience a conflict between diffidence and boldness, between our sense of unworthiness and our yearning to be
part of God's New Creation. "I waited"—vulnerable and shrinking

back in a sense of unworthiness—"But I could not wait." The violent inner urging toward Love just cannot be denied. And in the long run, it is the violent who bear it away.

Multitudes of mystics have testified to God's immanence, to the fact that no matter how we may feel about ourselves, we are in fact *never* far from God. When I accept that definition of things, I can perceive myself being transformed from a weak and limping palfrey to a horse with a spring in its step. What does it matter that as I trot across the field, some hint of my lameness remains in the tracks I leave upon the snow? The important thing is that I am turning my back on my old attitudes because the Christ-nature is being formed in me. As long as I am on the way and moving in the right direction, it does not matter that I am still imperfect. A limp now and then, an occasional slip-up, will not negate that I am on the grow.

And from the standpoint of eternity, the perfecting is already complete. From that standpoint, indeed, the unimportance of my ego-striving becomes fully evident. From that perspective, who can tell there was even a horse, let alone a lame one? Who can separate out the rider from the Ground of all Being? Who can distinguish the snow from the shimmer across its surface? The multiplicity of appearances becomes the organic unity of reality.

In the process of dying to ourselves and living to God, there is no percentage in focusing attention on our limp. Instead, "let us run with patience the race that is set before us, looking unto Jesus the author and finisher of our faith" (Hebrews 12:1–2).

The classical Greeks taught that a person became like whatever he or she thought about, looked at, and meditated on—hence the idealized beauty of their statues. Philippians 4:8 supports the same psychological principle by suggesting that people should think about "whatsoever things" are honest, just, pure, lovely, of good report, virtuous, and praiseworthy.

It is not only worthless but downright detrimental to concentrate on weaknesses and shortcomings, even our own. What is vital is to keep our minds focused on the Love we're already in.

William Paterson College, Thursday, 3:30 P.M.

Even if I could still
The clatter our voices make
On our way from the day's last class,
We could not surrender to each other
Our told-once-only tale of
Sole survival.
We are ourselves the campus mound
We cannot cross.
Yet some codes have been broken,
Like weather and the latest face of China,
And, after all, this place is habitat.
I want to sit right down here at home
In my own ill ease
And drink my tea on the lid
Of this quaint volcano.

MEDITATION

Martin Buber is only the first of the many philosophers, theologians, and psychologists who have taught us to distinguish between I-Thou and I-It relationships. Of course it is not possible to establish fully open intersubjective relationships with all the people we contact in a typical day. For a person to whom relationships are the very essence of significant living, that fact can be a bit disconcerting and can require a certain amount of adjustment. Since Catherine is a Professor of French at William Paterson College of New Jersey, this poem concerns adjustment to the patterns of relating at one's place of work.

The average colleague relationship is of necessity somewhat superficial. Hence the conversations during the walk from classrooms to the office building or the parking lot tend to be mere clatter. But even this variety of egobabble is not the real reason why we answer "Fine," no matter if our heart is breaking or our head is aching, when someone asks us how we are. It is simply not possible to open up the full range of our lives again and again. Indeed, even to our closest friend or lover, it is impossible to tell all the nuances of life as we have experienced it. Hence the tale of our sole survival is told only once—to our own Selves, in our deepest being.

Most of us are aware that it is self-important and counter productive to keep going on and on about our troubles to just anyone who will listen. It is this very awareness, as well as the inescapably solitary nature of the human center, that keeps the polite barrier standing between ourselves and our colleagues. Yet with at least some of them we have gotten beyond the codes of the most superficial discourse. Certainly we do more than comment on the state of the weather or the most recent newspaper headlines. For, after all, in a way the workplace is home. Unless we wish to relegate a large percentage of our working lives to limbo, we must live here and we must adapt here.

So, if we are wise, we learn to live as comfortably as possible with our own dis-ease and with the awareness that everyone around us has known trials at least as painful as our own. We can be confident that each person has survived sufficient anguish that if each of us tried to reveal our whole story, the entire place would erupt. So we learn to sit calmly on the lid of the volcano, drinking our tea.

~§ | Penitential Psalm

Street dogs still cock their ears,
Alley cats go taut in puzzlement,
Seas still hiss No, not now, Yes, now,
Koalas go on blinking at the zoo under morning:
You are not hidden.
Even street paper whirring like locusts
Has found you out
And dies for surprise
Into painted motion in flight and light.

Only I am forgotten by fear.
I never rise
With a cocked ear or a fur rod spine,
I am too used to the sea and to papers
Running in new feathers into the air.
I am asleep when night animals shudder
At the stare of day. Forgive.

MEDITATION

Walt Whitman was disturbed that people allow themselves to become deadened to the wonder of the "miraculous commonplace."
Looked at with fresh, pristine vision, he declared, "A mouse is
miracle enough to stagger sextillions of infidels." Folk wisdom has
expressed the deadening effect of taking people and events for
granted by the aphorism "Familiarity breeds contempt."

The speaker of "Penitential Psalm" asks God's forgiveness for failing to thrill to the sunrise. Although sunrise may be understood as God's presence within creation, it may also be understood simply as a natural phenomenon of great mystery and beauty, a phenomenon that would call forth tremendous awe if we had not become accustomed to it.

Many animals apparently possess the enviable gift of retaining fresh responses to natural phenomena. As the sun breaks the horizon, dogs may cock their ears, cats may stiffen, the sea hisses the time, the nocturnal bear-like Australian koala blinks in its zoo cage. None of these are dead to their environment. Even scrap paper on the street is responsive to the divine wonderment of the wind, whirling up in a miniature cyclone to image its surprised delight.

Only we human beings, it seems, tend to create walls of habit that block us from feeling alive. We are not visited by awe ("fear") because we allow our responses to become dull and blunted. We do not feel the human equivalent of a dog's cocking its ears or a cat's hair standing on end because of the arrival of the sun. (Indeed we customarily sleep right through that event; after all, it happens every day!) And we barely hear the message of the sea or notice the beauty of the whirling papers. In the best sense of the words, we are far from being too "materialistic" or "worldly." On the contrary, most of us are much too unresponsive to the textures and patterns and colors and events of the world we inhabit. We need to seek out the arts, to meditate, and to take time to feel in order to continually resensitize ourselves. If we don't, the loss is our own.

But if we can make any legitimate analogy between human artists and the Divine Artist, the loss is also God's. Anybody who has ever made a work of art can feel the pain of having that work greeted by a glassy, unseeing, unresponsive stare, or a careless shrug, or perhaps no glance at all. We do indeed owe God an apology. Forgive.

✒ | Right Now

"Chaque moment renferme donc tout."
—*de Caussade*

Sirens, shouts, and telephones,
Bells of death coming,
Wraith round and round you,
Zero heart-time.
You alone, charmed musical clock,
Toll with infinite slowness
And loose your limbs
With careless grace.

MEDITATION

"Each moment encloses everything." So wrote Jean-Pierre de Caussade, an eighteenth-century Jesuit and author of *Abandonment to Divine Providence*, regarded by many as the pinnacle of Roman Catholic mystical writing. His moment which encloses everything is of course something more than what we know as the space of a moment on our chronological clocks. It is a moment of "zero heart-time," which of course when it is experienced is always "right now." St. John referred to the realization of zero heart-time when he said, "Beloved, *now* are we the children of God" (1 John 3:2).

When the timepiece is the heart or center of human be-ing, the time is always zero: NOW, no-time, no-place, every-time, every-place, eternity, the place where numbers begin and end. Zero heart-time, otherwise known as the Eternal Now, occurs whenever we are so totally harmonious that we are functioning both in time and out of time (that is, in the timeless ultimate reality). In the latter dimension, our consciousness contains all that is, all that ever was, and all that ever will be. So the location of zero heart-time is always of necessity NOW/HERE.

Compared to the intense and all-encompassing reality of zero heart-time, things like sirens, shouts, and ringing telephones are only death knells, the pale ghosts of unreality. All of these natural and technological phenomena die quickly away because they are surrounded by competing phenomena. As human creatures we often feel distracted from one set of distractions by yet another set of them. But the charmed musical clock of zero heart-time is always relaxed and always attentive. Because foolishness is simply ignored in the Eternal Now, there is always time for what really matters. There is infinite time for infinite slowness and graceful freedom when we are dancing our part in the only dance there is.

⤠ | "Before I knew . . .
my heart had hurled me"
—Song of Songs

At first, feel of too far love:
Looking over your shoulder at the windows framing you.
Afterwards, sight of your coat piece by piece,
A cuff, a sleeve, a collar.
And then, the one curl on your neck
Holding my finger day and night.

MEDITATION

It is not enough to talk and think about God in an impersonal and abstract fashion, no matter how important that aspect of things may currently seem to be. We are attempting to break ourselves of the racist, classist, and sexist slant of our anthropormorphic concept of God as a rich white male grandfather in the sky. These attempts force us to cut down on the use of male pronouns and to stress feminine and neutral images of God as well as masculine ones. At this moment in history we desperately need to enlarge our concept of God and to serve human justice and all-inclusiveness in the way we speak of God. We need to remind ourselves that *all* our words about God are figures of speech that fall far short of reality and hence misrepresent God. Nevertheless, it would be a great loss indeed if all of that should rob our hearts of affectionate communion with an intensely personal God.

In the strangely paradoxical fashion that imbues all theological statement, God is both far more than an individual person and yet somehow is the essential Person. And although we worship

God in spirit, yet sensuous response may also be part of our inner communion.

Catherine describes such communion, taking her title from the Song of Solomon, that Hebrew masterpiece of sexual love which can also be read as describing the love between Christ and the soul. Following the idea that it is important sometimes to commune with one specific member of the Trinity, the speaker visualizes Christ Jesus. At first, the major feeling is great remoteness ("too far love") and a timid fear that this boldness may somehow be mistaken. What does it even *mean* to love God?

The speaker looks over Christ's shoulder at the windows against which he is silhouetted, afraid to look at him directly. Gradually, however, she begins to make out his coat: a cuff first, a sleeve, a collar. The coat image is taken from St. John of the Cross, who describes the coat of Christ as consisting of faith, hope, and charity.

But a coat is not the same as the person in it. Gradually gaining courage, the speaker moves close enough to touch a curl on Christ's neck. This image comes from Song of Solomon 4:9, where the bridegroom says to the bride, "Thou hast ravished my heart, my sister, my spouse; thou hast ravished my heart with one of thine eyes, with one chain [interpreted by Catherine as one curl] of thy neck."

But Catherine transposes the curl from the neck of the bride to the neck of the bridegroom. She also speaks of the curl's "Holding my finger day and night" instead of the finger's holding the curl, which would certainly make more sense on the literal level. Why these two transpositions, the curl from bride to groom, the holding from the bride's finger to the groom's curl? Two reasons: first, to emphasize the union between the lovers and the closeness of their identification. Second, to symbolize the fact that while prayer seems to be the human being seeking God (the finger holding the curl) even the disposition to seek communion with the divine Person comes from God and is sustained by God (the curl holding the finger).

We may often feel that we are hanging on to Christ. But in reality Christ is holding on to us holding on. And that's love. That's mutuality. That's security.

✒ | To Myself

I lived so long
With the fear of your dying
That my paws worried themselves away
Keeping the sand beneath your feet.
My face was wrinkled as a caryatid's
From holding the sky above your head.

That was in my youth
Which held out through two civilizations
Until I saw that, unshielded and unfragile,
You had already been crushed
By the sky into the ground.

The third long city passed
Saying goodbye to your stilled death
And amputated pain.

Now I'm in the fourth
Saying goodbye to goodbye.

MEDITATION

How do we relate to our own ego-consciousness, the personality that is called by our name yet is clearly not all there is to us? It is this external self, associated with our bodies, that is what we usually mean when we say "myself." And yet, we have also experienced movement into a deeper or larger Self wherein the concerns of that ego-self seem small, constricted, and short-sighted. (Is this what catharsis is all about, when our petty vision is purged through experiencing a great tragedy?) Such experiences tell us that our egos are not the whole definition of ourselves.

Still, there is that personality to which we must relate. Catherine's speaker in "To Myself" speaks out of the deepest Self to her superficial or body-oriented self. In the days of my youth, the speaker says, I utilized a great deal of energy worrying about the death of the ego-identity I had been battling so hard to establish. Would my individual personality and body be recognizably *me* after the resurrection, or would it be lost at death? And if I opened myself to the will of God here and now, would I lose my individuality?

Like the Sphinx, the speaker pawed at the desert sand of life, trying to put solid ground under the ego-nature. In terror of the unknown and terror of genuine autonomy with all of its responsibility, the speaker fought so hard to establish identity that she felt like one of the caryatids in the Acropolis, holding the sky upon her head. The burden of identity seemed all hers, and it was so heavy that her face wrinkled with stupendous effort.

Through the whole Egyptian and Greek civilizations, that effort was maintained. (Catherine is of course comparing the history of the speaker's relationship with her own ego-nature to the history of the world). What ended the sense of effort to assert and maintain separate identity was the realization that genuine identity had already been supplied. She no longer had to struggle to hold up the sky, because in point of fact the sky had long since crushed the ego into union with the ground (that is, its whole environment, including the body, the world, and the divine nature that upholds everything else). This realization brings with it the awareness that it is impossible to protect against the process of life and death. We can't do it. We're helpless before that process—"unshielded."

But we are also "unfragile." Despite our fears, God's grace has gifted us with strength, more strength than often we will believe we have.

A third phase of the redeemed Self's relationship to the self is trying to believe that we really have died to the old nature as an entity separated off from God, and really have been driven into union with the Ground of Being. People who have had an arm or leg amputated often report feeling pain in the member that is no longer there; similarly, the ego-nature often causes us pain even after we have died to it and come alive to the New Humanity. After a spiritual breakthrough, one of the worst temptations is to get discouraged when old habits reappear, habits we'd thought were gone forever as a result of that breakthrough. The temptation is to wonder whether the breakthrough ever occurred at all, or whether our spiritual growth is nothing but an illusion. It is a difficult spiritual discipline to say "goodbye" to the death of the self—to let go of the speculations surrounding it and simply believe it, and to refuse to be distracted by its "amputated pain."

But there is an even more advanced stage, a fourth "civilization," namely letting go even of the consciousness of one's spiritual progress. Instead of keeping score on our right hand of what our left hand is accomplishing, we can simply forget about ourselves by "saying goodbye to goodbye."

As our inner Sodom is crushed by the sky into the ground, we can spend a lot of time like Lot's wife, looking back at the scene of the purgation. Better far, however, is to learn not to bother looking back at ourselves looking at ourselves. We are new creatures: "old things are passed away; behold, all things are become new" (2 Corinthians 5:17). Even saying goodbye to the old nature is an authentication of its existence. Better to channel all our energies into the New Creation by simply "saying goodbye to goodbye."

❧ | My Home Non-Town, July

Only the farthest toe of the city probes my street,
So I spend the whole dawn
Tracking lawn tigers tracking.
It's time now the unicorns
Snorted down Route 23.
This morning Hermes will trim the back
With a polished hoof,
But North Cove afternoon
Is better for dreaming on the corded side
Of ooze.
In suburbia clues are harder,
But it makes for good fellowship
With passionate tabbies and manageable myths.

MEDITATION

"Grow where you're planted," says a slogan popular in religious
circles. Excellent advice it is, too, for some of us tend to be afflicted
with "the-grass-is-greener syndrome." Like Miniver Cheevy, we
think life might have been richer for us in another place and time.
Our own lives may appear rather drab compared to the flamboyance of tigers, unicorns, and winged messengers of classical and
medieval myths and legends. But we have to learn to live as gracefully as possible within our given environment. As Thomas Carlyle
said, if we are to build a cosmos out of our chaos, the place we
must begin to build is here—here or nowhere.

Catherine's milieu happens to be Wayne, New Jersey, part of the sprawling suburbs of New York and the Clifton/Paterson/Newark urban complex. Route 23, "the farthest toe of the city," intersects the street Catherine lives on.

Even in prosaic Wayne, New Jersey, romance is a matter of perception. For a lively imagination, ordinary cats prowling the yard can transform themselves into lawn tigers, and the cars and trucks on busy Route 23 become snorting unicorns. The youngster who trims the back yard becomes Hermes (otherwise known as Mercury), the messenger of the gods and the keeper of their cattle.

North Cove, a local lake used for public swimming, provides a metaphor for the mythic limitations of suburban life. There is an area corded off for children and swimmers, beyond which the lake bottom becomes much more primordial, full of muddy slime. Although the ooze might make an ideal setting for romantic tales of knights and dragons, the bathing beach on the corded side is a better place for comfortable fantasizing and dreaming. Similarly, romance may be harder to come by in suburia, but the myths are easier to control—somewhat tamed, scaled-down, but also more familiar, less threatening, more manageable. Tabby cats may not be as exciting as tigers, but they have their passions too, and they are a whole lot safer to handle. To lose one virtue, therefore, is to gain another.

The spot where the grass is greenest is not the other side of the fence. It's located wherever the contented eye can see green and respond to it.

◆§ | The Way It Was. How Shall It Be?

Do you know what it is
To dream the light-tree growing
In some all over the place and persistence?
It is an ever wound to see
In the same breath
Green, high noon, and surmise.
It ruined me forever
For lamplight and evening fire
And that too slow laugh
Under visible elms.

MEDITATION

The Greeks had many myths warning that once a man had experienced intercourse with a goddess, he was ruined forever for relationships with women of ordinary humanity. English poet John Keats immortalized one such myth in his "La Belle Dame Sans Merci," which begins, "O what can ail thee, knight-at-arms, alone and palely loitering?" It turns out that what ails the knight is yearning for a goddess he has known one time, who was merciless in that she returned to her divine realm. She left him forever eating his heart out for a being who cannot ever become part of his daily life.

Such passionate longing is only one relatively "adolescent" stage of spiritual growth, or, viewed from another angle, only one aspect of mature religious experience. Yet when a person's heart is fixed in Paradise Regained, sometimes the upside-down values of the world we live in will make difficult any mature enjoyment of

Eternity Now. Like Paul, we may sometimes ache to "be with Christ, which is far better" (Philippians 1:23). It is this longing for a once-glimpsed perfection that Catherine describes in "The Way It Was. How Shall It Be?"

The way the vision was, was that a tree of light grew "all over the place" and persisted all the time, so that the tree was everyplace and everytime. At the same single second, the speaker could see all stages of the light-tree's existence: the green beginnings, the high noon of the present moment, and the future ("surmise"). And this brilliant vision ruined her forever for the more mundane lights of lamps and evening fires, and for pleasant laughter under ordinary ("visible") trees. She is, as Eliot worded it, "no longer at ease here/ In the old dispensation/ With an alien people clutching their gods."

The dissatisfaction with ordinary humanity is only one phase (often recurrent) of the spiritual quest. Fortunately for us all, another phase is the return to appreciating domestic tranquility. But there *are* those times, at least for mystical visionaries, when one is too distracted by glimpses of another realm of reality to feel satisfied with the everyday world.

That's the way it was. How shall it be? More wonderful, surely, than any glimpse could have prepared us for. Since our end is our beginning, we need not fear our times of divine dissatisfaction. After all, they serve to point us toward the glory that shall be.

✍ | The Smile

Trackless as the quit life of shells
You well may be,
But it took only the time
It takes a wave to mirror-flash
The light on its roar
At day come again
For me to catch your smile
Before we quit each other
At this morning's door.

No smile ever said goodbye
And come in just that way.
That kind of smile belongs
In sea-air lighted
Or, as I shall remember
At this evening's window,
In warm rooms with views
Of rooftops fading
Moments before sleep.

MEDITATION

These days church people are talking a lot about the issue of sexual
fidelity. Medical advances have vastly lengthened the human life-
span, so that a lifelong marriage or love-commitment is now liable
to span a period of fifty or more years. In former eras, when women

frequently gave their lives in childbirth and people were old in their fifties, and when marriage was understood more as an efficient social arrangement than as a meaningful personal relationship, obviously the issue of fidelity was not as intense as it is today. Many people are asking whether it is even possible to preserve freshness and variety in a daily live-in relationship that spans several decades. If it is, they want to know how.

In "The Smile," Catherine suggests one very important way to avoid dullness and boredom: to learn to pay attention to the infinite nuances in the personality of the other as he or she grows and changes through the years. In the first place, it is the height of foolishness to think that anyone could ever come to the end of knowing another person. Any human personality is full of mystery, as free of tracks as an empty shell. For those who learn to appreciate that mystery and to enjoy watching whatever hints emerge from the other, a lifetime is too short for learning all there is to know.

But in the meantime, on the daily basis, there are many superbly familiar moments, flashes of intimacy, such as a goodbye smile at the door on the way to work. Just as it takes waves only a split second to flash reflections of the rising sun, it takes human beings only a split second to flash to each other a totally unique expression of love. The waves do not make their own light, but merely lend their surface to reflect a light beyond themselves. Similarly, a long-loved smile reflects all the history of the constantly growing relationship in all of its combined mysteries. As the years pass, that smile can only grow more rich.

No smile in the world is ever just like any other smile. But the smiles of parting and greeting that are smiled by the one with whom one shares a life-commitment carry with them an unconditional acceptance that makes them eternally new. If they belong in any category at all, they belong to the category of fresh ocean air at dawn. Or to the category of drowsy bedrooms: quiet, steady, full of trust. There is security in such a smile, but there is no boredom.

ᴥ | The Purpose of Dying Capitalism

Catch the letters
As they fall
Between the memos
Of the frog-prince.
Steal electric snow
At the check-out counter
In between the snap of bags.
Walk around the house
Recycling amoebas from the dust.
If they put you in a nursing home,
Scoop up the silent, secret howl
Under your uncut nail.
The purpose of dying capitalism
     for consumer poets
Is to hoard.

MEDITATION

People who think much about the meaning of their lives sooner or
later have to wonder why they were born into precisely this period
of history rather than any other, this place rather than any other.
For instance, a middle-class suburban American woman must wonder why she finds herself living in a patriarchal system in which
she and others like her are definitely not at the top of the heap.
Looking around her, she sees that capitalism cannot continue for

long, at least not in the form it currently assumes. So crying are the injustices to the poor that something has got to give. How do we cope as positively as we can with the historical conditions in which we have been placed?

Well: for one thing, we must learn to glean whatever little meaning we can find in the ninety percent of nonsense we have to read at our place of work. The men who write the self-inflated memos within our patriarchal structures are "frog-princes." They too are victims; they are the oppressors imprisoned by an oppressive system just as surely as those they help to oppress. There doubtless are princes hidden inside those frogs, but they will never appear without a very specific liberation! (For the poor, liberation is from physical need; but for rich frog-princes, liberation must be from self-important power and money).

Secondly, we who are trying to survive with significance must somehow seek the human/divine dimension in really unlikely places like supermarket check-out counters. Snow is "electric" because it is living, vibrant, natural reality. The question is, can we learn how to give ourselves such vibrancy even within frustrating routine? Can we learn to keep in tune with the cosmos even amidst the snapping of grocery bags?

And third, we must learn to see life in what we formerly regarded as merely inorganic ugliness. If everything that lives is really holy, that would include even amoebas . . . and they in turn would dignify even the dust!

All of this is to say that under our less-than-optimal conditions we must learn to experience reality as fully as possible, despite our inevitable pain. If we wind up in a nursing home, then that must become our real world, and our function will be to feel all the accumulated anguish of the place. For anguish is a sign of life.

In short, for "consumer poets" who are doing the best they can to live significantly with little or no share of the power, the purpose of dying capitalism is (ironically) to hoard. The hoarding is not of material goods, however, but of reality. The poet—meaning anyone who is not entirely controlled by technology—attempts everywhere to find and preserve the living essence beneath routine appearances. Although capitalism subsists on the hoarding of those who consume its products, there is really only one thing *worth* "hoarding." It is worth hoarding precisely because, like manna, it can never be possessed and therefore can never literally be hoarded: the authentic, organic life of the spirit wherever it may be found.

৶ | Between the Bearing and the Borne

I have no child at all.
But time persists in crying
Mother-father to me.

What, who shall ever
Bring me up to be?
But moment just won't stop playing
At parenting me.

Time, day after night,
Turns dark and light to liquid
In my open throat.

And moment is always busy
Letting me know
How long my heart can go on gently.

MEDITATION

Sir Thomas Browne, a seventeenth-century physician and author, spoke of humanity as amphibian, since we function simultaneously in time and eternity. It is this amphibious status that Catherine explores in "Between the Bearing and the Borne."

In relationship to time, a human being is the parent, the bearing. It is the human consciousness that gave birth to the clock, the alphabet, and the whole concept of chronological measurement. But in relationship to the Eternal Now ("moment"), the human being is the child, the borne. We came out of the eternal present tense, we live our measured hours in present tense surrounded by past and future, and we return to the eternal present tense—not only as individuals but also as an entire human family. For as Sir Thomas also said, "Time is but a short parenthesis in a long period [sentence]".

Eternity parents us throughout our infinitesimally short appearance within time's short parenthesis. Only when we have passed out of the parenthesis and into the surrounding sentence will we be fully grown, complete, able simply to *be* (as opposed to constantly moving along in process).

Time, which imprisons us all our lives, presses relentlessly forward, melding into a stream or flow of nights and days. Wise human beings try to keep an open throat toward time's liquid, hoping not to close out any aspect of reality. Meanwhile, the Eternal Now is always part of our consciousness, reminding us that it is still possible for us to submit to God, to abandon ourselves to life, to go on. Like a kind parent, eternity schools us lovingly rather than harshly. For that reason, we who are conscious of our amphibian status can sense that our hearts beat gently, never in desperation. And so we live, parents of time and children of eternity, until our hearts cease gently from their gentle beating.

ᴥᔥ | Back Entry

Contrary to my look,
I have not come back from the dead.
From wonder, I turned around in flight
Without becoming salt.

I have not left you:
Only, seeing you from the back,
I'm stumbling backwards now
Over every sing-song hill.

I have not left you:
In every town I see recede,
There is still a school
And wars drawn up and down to scale.
It's true my way's no way to win a race,
But the back of my heel
Will touch the land's end first,
And when I lift my left foot there,
I'll pull all of you with me into the sea.

MEDITATION

The speaker in "Back Entry" is someone who is running backwards, facing this life in an attempt to alert humanity to life's deeper dimensions while moving rapidly toward the sea of eternity. Since her back is to the ocean and her face toward the land, she may look as if she is returning from the dead. But she explains that, no, that is not the case. She was living life in the usual way (frontwards) when she became aware of imminent death and turned around to view the concerns of life from that strong awareness. ("From Wonder" she turned, not from vulgar curiosity.) Because her motives differ from those of Lot's wife, she is not turned to a pillar of salt but rather combines continued flight with consciousness-raising by running backwards.

She has not left the land of the living, she explains, but she sees life from a different angle ("seeing you from the back"), from the dimension of eternity instead of from absorption in time. Stumbling backwards through life's routine ups and downs, she sees that despite the witness she tries to make, life is going on in its self-destructive way, with schools still teaching about battles as if warfare were life's zenith.

Eventually the backwards race across the land will reach the seashore. When she slips into the ocean of eternity, she hopes to pull the living with her into a deeper spiritual awareness, accomplishing in death whatever she has not been able to accomplish in life.

Titus 2:14 speaks of Christians as "a peculiar people, zealous of good works." Yet in our day, there are precious few Christians who have any distinguishing marks about our lifestyles to set us in counterdistinction to the rest of the world. Too many of us are competing in the worldly race of getting and spending, so that our faith seems little more than a pious overlay to life. Our face is set in the same direction as everyone else's, since we are all running toward the same goals. Catherine has provided us with a metaphor for what the Christian *disciple's* presence is in the world: running against the crowd, appearing to step out of eternity as a representative of eternal values, backing away from ego-entanglements all the while we are witnessing to a more spiritual consciousness. If we live that kind of life, perhaps in some mysterious way at the moment of death we will indeed be used to increase the consciousness of the people who have known about our way of dying into life.

✺ | Our Three Birches Are Dead

Three little trees outside my house
Are dead at my expense.
But at least my passion is peat,
If not yet diamond.
In the space of a month or two,
Tree and tree and tree
Fell into my nose and ears and eyes,
Stumbling like children
Waked to a night
Of coal hard dream.

MEDITATION

Many of us have at one time or another felt angry at the very idea that growth is promoted by suffering. And yet we have not been able to deny that fact, for we have seen people grow more gentle, humble, open, and vulnerable as the result of the turmoil in their lives. Even the Bible bears witness to pain as a producer of beauty, telling us that God chose to make the captain of our salvation perfect through suffering (Hebrews 2:10). Like it or not, there it is.

The speaker in "Our Three Birches Are Dead" had purchased and planted in her yard three little trees which she grew to love very much. When they died, she experienced grief, for in a sense they had been like children to her. At the moment the poem is spoken, considerable time has lapsed since the death of the trees. When first they died, the pain she felt was certainly not so pure and transparent and reflective of the light as a diamond; yet at least it was peat, the first step toward the making of a diamond.

As the months passed by, she did not forget about the trees. Rather, they became interiorized ("fell into my nose and ears and eyes"). Dreaming about the trees and all they symbolized to her, along with the pressure of grieving for their loss, hardens the original peat-sorrow into coal. Coal is not yet diamond, of course: not yet perfect through suffering, but at least moving in the right direction.

Sometimes we seem to have very little choice about what happens to us. But our freedom of will always has its opportunity in the way we *receive* what happens to us. Will we rage and reject and try to forget what does not feel good to us? Or will we take the peat of ordinary or extraordinary sorrow, perhaps put it under the pressure of examination until it yields the coal of insight, and certainly absorb it as part of our whole life-offering to a God of Living Reality who knows our best interests far more thoroughly than we ourselves know them? Only that kind of pressure can yield a diamond.

The Virgin Mary enunciated the principle that turns peat into coal into diamond: "Be it unto me according to thy will." Others since have said it in other ways. For instance, twentieth-century missionary martyr Jim Elliot wrote in his diary shortly before his death, "It is not necessary that I live. It is only necessary that the will of God be done." And three centuries earlier, Sir Thomas Browne concluded *Religio Medici* with the words, "[God's] will be done, though in my own undoing."

Sometimes, however, it is easier to make sweeping statements like these when all is well, than to accept the everyday frustrations everyone must endure. The pressure that creates a diamond may build up out of a combination of little griefs. Not the heroic measures, but the "little foxes that spoil the vines": these are the test of yieldedness. Like, for instance, the death of three little birch trees.

❧ | And You Shall Go In and Out and Shall Find Pastures

If in this life
There are pastures,
Then what is in,
And what is out?

In the economy
Of wonder,
What I eat feeds you,
What you eat feeds me.

Then, as we live,
Out is in
And in is out.
But a lonely thing
It is
Never to taste
The blades we chew.

MEDITATION

To his disciples and a group of Pharisees Jesus said, "I am the door: by me if any . . . [one] enter in, he [or she] shall be saved, and shall go in and out, and find pasture" (John 10:9). Pondering the meaning of that statement, Catherine asks, since going *in* through the door of Christ seems to imply security for now and all eternity, and going *out* through the same door means finding nourishment in the pastures of God, which are apparently located in this earthly life, what is *in* and what is *out*? How is it possible to make such a distinction?

In the system or economy of mystery and eternal essence ("wonder"), we human beings are so whole and undivided that whatever strength we gain strengthens everyone else, and whatever growth others achieve helps bring us toward maturity. Even in the privacy of our own homes, living lovingly is nourishment that spiritually feeds the whole universe we live in. (It does not, however, *physically* feed the eight hundred million hungry people of the earth, and that too is part of our responsibility.) Aware of our need for grace and repentant about our involvement in systemic evil, we must still see to it that the energy we transmit is positive and contented, not bitter and negative.

If we associate the words "out" and "in" with traditional concepts, going "in" would refer to closeness to God, eternity, and the spirit, while going "out" would refer to time and the body. Whereas traditionalists have always valued eternity over time and spirit over body, Jesus seems to be smashing that hierarchal notion. "Out is in/ And in is out," according to his definition of things. So the split between body and spirit is healed at the door which is Christ's Body. Accordingly, the responsibility for our sisters and brothers is a physical as well as spiritual one.

Nevertheless, no matter how fully we may believe in the mystical unity of the Body and the wholistic, organic oneness of our physical and spiritual life, a problem remains. Somehow the intellectual belief never can be fully experienced on our pulses. The sense of our Ultimate Oneness is elusive, always just a bit beyond our practical enjoyment. We know, and yet we do not know. Even though we are nourished and are giving nourishment with the blades of grass we chew in God's pasture, we can never quite *taste* them. We can go "in" to find the strength to come back "out" into the frustrating incompleteness and ambiguity of the human condition. We can be very grateful that when we go "out," we find pastures. Despite all that, however, it's lonely out here.

✌ | Questions on Profane and Sacred Love

Though lovers pattern love,
What have round and round kisses
To do with the still sun?
Or should we think of lovers
As simple pharaohs of the heart
Entombed as lessons to us all
Of doomed persistence?

Can loves where words are still just possible
Speak of word-doomed love?
Is the long distance between the kiss and
    the telling of it
Like the doomed pit between any word
    and the sun?

MEDITATION

It is commonplace that human lovers give us some sense of what union with the Divine Lover is all about. Perhaps that is one reason why "all the world loves a lover." Certainly mystics have frequently used sexual figures of speech to try to share some glimpse of their experience of oneness with God.

But just what *is* the relationship between the dynamic, eager, fluctuating drive of human sexual passion and the changelessness of eternal love? Is there any real way to define the relationship positively? Or is the equation as negative as John Keats assumed it to be? Looking at a Grecian urn, he said that the bas-relief lover, frozen in the second before a kiss, is far more fortunate than the living lover who eventually must become sated. To Keats the eternal silence of the lovers captured in art's eternity is far preferable to "All breathing human passion . . . that leaves a heart high-sorrowful and cloyed,/ A burning forehead, and a parching tongue."

Perhaps, though, negating ordinary love in favor of the eternal is not the right approach to this question. Perhaps we should think of "profane" lovers as if they were ancient and entombed rulers. They may be dead by comparison to God's love, but by their persistent efforts to make love work, they teach us something about communion with God. As the author of *The Cloud of Unknowing* implied, it is only by the persistence of our desire that we can pierce the cloud in which God dwells.

But maybe it is altogether a mistake to try to define in words a relationship that can only be intuited. Since even human lovers cannot comprehend each other fully, love between them is love "where words are still just [barely] possible." By comparison, love between creature and Creator is utterly "word-doomed," impossible to speak about, ineffable. Can the nearly wordless be expected to say something about the totally silent?

Consider, for instance, the difference between experiencing a lover's kiss and describing it or hearing about it. There is a relationship of some sort, certainly, but the gap is enormous. And consider the difference between any scientific description of the sun and the sun itself. . . .

The rest is silence.

❧ | To God as Pantagruel

What I want is justice for you.
You deserve better than to be a face
Filtered through the recyclers of my mind.
I am very frightened, too,
Of pitting muteness against your silence.
I need, but have no right,
To defend your innocence of any speech—
You with your tongue of licking lava
And a mouth as gaping as the planet.
But no smooth case by a recycling spark
In the dancing reeds is possible.
At least, opening my mouth for you
Is a little better than injustice,
And enough to justify my own crossing
And recrossing on your lower lip
That dances, too, once in a while.

MEDITATION

Pantagruel, the chief character in Rabelais' satire *Gargantua and Pantagruel*, was so strong that he had to be chained into his cradle. But he broke the chains into five hundred thousand pieces with one blow of his infant fist. As a man, he knew all languages, all sciences, and all knowledge of every sort. The last of the great giants, he could shelter an entire army under his tongue, and his throat and mouth contained whole cities. In addition to his size, strength, and knowledge, he was famous for two things: being even wiser than King Solomon and indulging in coarse, boisterous humor.

Catherine speaks to God in the image of Pantagruel, imagining herself living on his lower lip and trying to justify her own existence by justifying God's. God as the all-encompassing universe, with a mouth as huge as the whole world, remains silent when charges are brought against him. Sometimes poets would like to defend him. But a poet is after all only a dancing reed instrument, recycling ideas like sparks of light—transitory, repetitive, vulnerable. A poet really has no right to play God's defense attorney, and certainly no smooth, airtight case can be made for a silent sprawling giant of a God. If Milton dared to write *Paradise Lost* "to justify the ways of God to man," he was only the most distinguished in the long line of dancing reeds who have made that attempt.

Catherine wants for God something more fair than merely being made in some image her limited mind can dream up. She would like to give God greater justice than merely to recyle some theologian's or artist's concept of God (yet paradoxically that is just what she is doing with Rabelais). Despite her concern about human limitations, she tries to image God anyway, because she is afraid simply to say nothing. She needs to defend God, even if she has no right and no real abililty to do so. At least to attempt to speak in God's defense, however ineptly, is better than to do the injustice of saying nothing at all.

So much for all the theological, philosophical and artistic statements that have ever been devised to defend God! The efforts by dancing reeds are honorable in their intentions and perhaps in their execution. But they can do very little justice to God. Fortunately, God has a rich sense of humor. His lip "dances, too, once in a while."

For an Aging Friend

Why should a young man running
Figure cresting beauty
And make the old man weep
    for something lost?
No, it is you, old man, who figures
A young man running forever.
Even if you die before me,
The one I will see, I see.

MEDITATION

We live in a youth culture. As the average age of the American population increases, the adulation of looking, thinking and behaving "young" grows ever more frantic. The ideal embodiment or depiction of beauty is either the curvacious bathing queen or the athletic young man in jogging shorts. It is enough to make old people cry for all that they have lost. Although William Wordsworth consoles himself that his advancing years have brought him the "abundant recompense" of the "philosophic mind" that is able to hear "the still, sad music of humanity," such a recompense seems anything but abundant to anyone who has accepted the self-image peddled by Madison Avenue.

Catherine writes to a wise and spiritual elderly friend that it is he who provides the norm for the young man, not the other way around. Thus, like Browning, she defines old age as "the last of life, for which the first was made."

More than that: she already is able to see beyond the wrinkles and the stiffening joints to the perfect resurrection body of her friend. Even should he die before her, she has already seen in the excellence of his life the "cresting beauty" of his immortal form. The one she will see in heaven, she already sees.

"The path of the just is as a shining light, that shineth more and more unto the perfect day" (Proverbs 4:18). The old age of a spiritual person who has spent life running for the immortal garland is best summarized, not as decrepitude, but as an eternal youth running tirelessly forever.

Postcard from Palermo

Tourists from the catacombe cappucini
Sway from cumulus cloud hooks
Along the sky wall from Palermo to Charybdis.
Baron, whose morning coat outlives your skin,
Green-checked stick girl who cannot now forgive him,
How much more private, baron, simple bones are;
Serva, how much sweeter revenge to leave
   no trace at all.
Why did you punish them, cappucini,
Leaving tamed Cerberus at the door
And Charon in sandals, collecting the coin of entry?
Who are these titans that cross Messina with me,
Reminding me of deaths I died myself
Running through lava olive fields
Over Tartarus and under Etna.
Shall these green checks and lace cuffs live?

All of us are moving forever from living to alive.
Some are soon alive, some now,
Some with the first wakening of the stopped heart.
Some still clothed shells tell us
Some must wait to see it is already done.

MEDITATION

Palermo is, of course, the capital of Sicily, and one of its most prized tourist stops is the catacomb established by nineteenth-century Capuchin monks. Located in a vast crypt under a church, the "catacombe cappucini" feature the bodies of human beings, fully clothed, most of them hanging from hooks but some preserved in glass coffins. The corpses are neatly arranged in rows according to their occupations: a row of lawyers, physicians, barons, nobles, babies, and so forth. The dry air of the crypt preserves the bodies in various stages of decomposition, and the costumes are usually perfectly preserved. Although the last burial took place in 1920, one child in a glass coffin looks as if she might have died just yesterday. Her picture is on a postcard that is one of the best-sellers among tourists to Palermo.

After her visit to the Catacombe Cappucini, Catherine looks at her fellow-tourists as they travel across the Strait of Messina, the body of water immortalized by Homer as the dangerous passage between Scylla and Charybdis. Her imagination dominated by what she has just seen, Catherine imagines the tourists dangling from hooks in the clouds. One tourist reminds her of the baron in the catacomb whose skin is partially rotted while his morning coat has continued in good condition. Another tourist brings to mind a skeleton wearing a green-checked dress. Catherine considers this serving-woman ("serva") much more fortunate than the baron she might have served and resented, since a skeleton preserves more privacy than a partially recognizable face.

And Catherine wonders what every sensitive person who tours this catacomb must wonder: why did the Capuchin monks choose to punish these people by robbing them of the privacy and dignity of the grave?

The door to the crypt is guarded by two Franciscan (Capuchin) friars who like Cerberus and Charon collect the entrance fee. In classical myth Cerberus is the three-headed dog whose job is to guard the entrance to the infernal regions. Charon is the one who ferries the spirit across the River Styx to the Elysian Fields. The ancient Greeks always placed a coin in the mouth or hand of the dead in order to pay Charon and a cake to placate Cerberus. So as the tourists pay their entrance fee into the land of the dead, they prefigure their own entrance into eternity.

As Catherine crosses the Strait of Messina, she cannot forget the corpses she has seen. They ride with her, and she feels united with them in their lives and in their deaths. In her imagination she runs with them across the fields beneath Etna, the volcano, and above Tartarus, the hell where the Titans were confined, thought to be located beneath central Sicily. Thinking of the row upon row of clothed cadavers and skeletons, she asks herself the question the Lord asked Ezekiel in the valley of dry bones: "Son of man, can these bones live?"

The response her heart gives her is contained in the final stanza. As surely as we are all naked under our clothes, we are all skeletons under our skin and spiritual beings under our skeletons. All of us are moving on a spiritual quest toward death, when we will begin to be fully alive. The death-that-brings-life can come to us at any time when we agree to be born again into Christ, the New Humanity: or it will certainly come at physical death, when some people will see for the first time that eternity is not simply a myth.

Henry David Thoreau commented that he had rarely met a person who was fully awake. Catherine classifies human beings similarly, according to our relationship to life and death. As if she were observing the corpses classified according to occupation and lifestyle, she classifies her contemporaries. Some of us are soon to die into life (be "soon alive"); we are close to *metanoia* or conversion. Some of us are maturely alive already, long before physical death, because we are dead to any notion of individual separateness and profoundly alive to spiritual wholeness. Some of us are just recently come alive through death, and are experiencing the first spiritual insights of the heart that no longer imagines itself unique and separate. And some of us, alas, are only the clothed shells of humanity, not at all aware of our spiritual dimension and not likely to become aware until we have experienced the death of our bodies. It is this latter group which makes clear that for some people, the reconciliation with God in our deepest Selves—the reconciliation that was meant to brighten all of life—will never be perceived as real until after life is over.

We are, all of us, hanging by hooks from the clouds. The big question is, which row are we hanging in?